'Jenny Baker's *Equals* is as lively as it is profound, and as practical as it is idealistic. She paints a powerful vision of a world where both women and men are strengthened and freed by the practice of true equality, and offers us positive and encouraging examples and ideas to help us imagine how to get from here to there. This book won't just make you want to change your life, it will tell you how.'

*Steve Holmes, Senior Lecturer in Theology, University of St Andrews*

'What I love about Jenny is how honouring and encouraging she is towards both men and women . . . My hope is that we can see future leaders catch on early to the freedom and fullness of living in equality that [*Equals*] so brilliantly articulates.'

*Miriam Swaffield, Student Mission Developer at Fusion UK*

'[*Equals*] will prove really helpful for couples looking to 'do life' on the basis of equality rather than power.'

*David Westlake, Integral Mission Director, Tearfund*

'Jenny Baker doesn't just teach on equality – she thoroughly lives it out. This book provides a much needed challenge for Christians to rethink the complex issues of gender and to restore people to their God-ordained equality and freedom.'

*Vicky Beeching, writer and broadcaster*

'This is a bold and beautiful book on a key issue. Jenny has read widely and reflected deeply, and draws on insights from many different disciplines to argue that when women and men regard one another equally, both are enabled to reach their full potential – an idea that is backed up by loads of practical examples, all of them illustrated by personal stories and informed by her own Christian faith.'

*Professor John Drane, theologian and author*

'Jenny Baker clearly presents her case that gender equality is not about eliminating difference, nor about diminishing men in order to promote women, but about rethinking traditional roles so that every person fulfils their true potential. With her characteristic warmth and wisdom, she offers research and experience, stories and statistics, to show that at work, in society, at home, and in the Church, egalitarian relationships are not a threat, but the promise of a better world in which men and women flourish.'

*Maggi Dawn, author and Professor of Theology and Literature, University of Yale*

'Jenny is without a doubt one of the foremost thinkers and commentators on the issues of faith and gender. You may not agree with all she says but I guarantee that you will be hugely challenged and enriched by engaging with this book. Whatever your stance on this key area you simply must read this much needed contribution to the debate.'

*Carl Beech, General Director, Christian Vision for Men*

Jenny Baker has been an advocate and activist for the equality of men and women for many years. She has spoken about gender equality in various contexts, and is a host of the Gathering of Women Leaders in London. She has an MSc in Gender Studies and is an accomplished author. Jenny works as Development Manager at Church Urban Fund, and is a marathon runner and keen cyclist. www.jennybaker.org.uk

# EQUALS

*Enjoying gender equality
in all areas of life*

Jenny Baker

First published in Great Britain in 2014

Society for Promoting Christian Knowledge
36 Causton Street
London SW1P 4ST
www.spckpublishing.co.uk

*British Library Cataloguing-in-Publication Data*
A catalogue record for this book is available from the British Library

ISBN 978–0–281–07069–5
eBook ISBN 978–0–281–07070–1

Typeset by Graphicraft Limited, Hong Kong
First printed in Great Britain by Ashford Colour Press
Subsequently digitally printed in Great Britain

eBook by Graphicraft Limited, Hong Kong

Produced on paper from sustainable forests

*For Jonny*
*I couldn't have done this without you*

# Contents

# Acknowledgements

Thank you to Audrey for your courage in challenging the status quo at Crabtree Lane Chapel. Thank you to Richard and Janice Russell, and Anne and Mark Burghgraefe-Rocque who led life-changing Bible studies at St Matt's in Bath and helped us to think theologically. Thank you to Chrissie and Gerard Kelly for early conversations about equality and all you have modelled. Thank you to Lowell Sheppard, John Buckeridge, Dave Wiles and Jon Birch for the encouragement and opportunities you gave me. Thank you to the talented and determined women who have inspired and accompanied me, including Wendy Beech-Ward, Lauretta Wilson, Julia Wickham, Anna Poulson, Rachel Gardner, Julie Johnson, Virginia Luckett and Esther Baker. Thank you to Roger Foster-Smith for investing in the Sophia Network which gave me the opportunity to develop a lot of my thinking. Thank you to my dad and mum, Ian and Mary Slark, for your amazing example of partnership, love and faithfulness in your marriage. Thank you to Joel and Harry for not only surviving our experiment of shared parenting but being incredibly talented and wonderful men. Thank you to Jonny Baker for sharing life with me. All of you have contributed to this book in different ways, for which I am very grateful.

A book is never written in isolation. Thank you to Alison Barr and all at SPCK for your work in editing and publishing this book. Thank you to Godfrey Rust and Nanda Griffeon for conversations about equality while running. Thank you to everyone who provided examples of practising equality, particularly Miriam Swaffield, Ruth Wells, Sonia Mainstone Cotton, Fran Walsh, Bridget and Nick Shepherd, Clare and Jon Birch, Caroline Bretherton, Neil Roper, Lisa Raine Hunt, Martin Saunders, Vicky Walker, Lis Baraka, Linda Fisher-Hoyrem, Su Blanch, Matt Summerfield,

## Acknowledgements

Malcolm Duncan, Mark Greene, Sharon Prior, Lowell Sheppard and Sarah Sharpe. Thank you to friends who commented on early drafts, especially Virginia Luckett whose honesty made this a much better book, and Jonny Baker whose wisdom made it a lot shorter.

# Introduction

I was brought up in the Brethren Church, where men made decisions and women made the tea. One Sunday morning, during the breaking of bread service, a woman called Audrey stood up and started reading the story of Rahab from the Bible. A number of people hurriedly left in protest, chairs scraping as they went, with Audrey raising her voice to be heard. When she reached the end of the passage, she started to say something about it, 'This was a woman . . .', only for one of the elders to say, 'That's enough, dear.' Her courage failed her and she sat down. The aftermath was horrible: a tense atmosphere, another elder saying something to try and draw people together, small groups of people talking urgently afterwards about how to address the problem. It felt like something terrible had happened. I had just accepted that men and women had different roles to play, with women being silent in public but influential behind the scenes; this was the first time anyone had challenged that and it felt very uncomfortable.

But it did get me thinking. The people at the church were God-fearing and Bible-believing, but their vision of the way life should be organized between men and women was in stark contrast to the stirring sense in my spirit that somewhere within me was a leader waiting to emerge. During my teenage years I swung like a pendulum between thinking 'If that's what God wants for women, then I don't want anything to do with God,' and 'If that's what God wants, then that's what I'll become.' When I got to know Jonny at university, it seemed even more important to sort it out. I read books on Christian marriage that I ended up throwing at the wall. Did we need to squeeze ourselves into these patterns of behaving that didn't come naturally, or could we both somehow be ourselves, develop our gifts and work things out between us?

We started asking questions at our church, St Matthew's in Bath, and the vicar and his wife organized a series of Bible studies. We discovered a liberating theology of the whole of life redeemed, including relationships between men and women, and a very different understanding of what the Bible said about women and men. Jonny and I got married and set out to do life together, committing to share everything equally, including work, parenting, housework, and the challenge of working out our callings. We were able to job-share when our boys were little and so also shared hands-on parenting. Now our boys are men and seem to have survived the experiment very well.

In the UK, where only a fifth of MPs are female, where women are paid less than men and one in four will experience violence from their partner, where men comprise the vast majority of the prison population and boys are underperforming at school, that biblical vision of the full equality of women and men is needed now more than ever. It seems to me that the Church should be leading the way, with restored relationships between men and women because of the amazing redemption that Jesus brings to every area of life, but instead we're still arguing over women bishops and male headship. I thought we would have sorted all that out by now.

There is no blueprint for sharing life more equally but I hope that this book will provoke many discussions about how it might be done so that both women and men can thrive. More than that, I hope that it will be a catalyst for some creative explorations for doing life together differently, creating communities and churches where the fantastic diversity of women and men is released and celebrated, and the liberating truth of Christ's redemption is experienced.

## Some things to note

There is always more that could be written on a subject. This is a book about men and women which talks primarily about heterosexual relationships. I know that life is more richly complex than that, that not everyone fits into a neat gender binary and that there's an urgent need for Christians to understand issues of equality and sexuality. I don't think I'm the person to write on those issues, not because I don't care about them but because I know and have experienced too little.

This book is written on the foundation of an egalitarian[1] theology. As an evangelical in my early twenties, it was really important for me to study the biblical material on women and men, to understand how to interpret it, and to realize that what I had imbibed as a teenager was not the only or the most accurate way of understanding the texts. Not all Christians feel the need to justify their passion for equality with their reading of the Bible, but if you are from a tradition that does I would encourage you to do that work.

# 1

## Exploring equality

———•◦•———

One hundred years ago, Emily Davison fought hard for women to have the right to vote. She was jailed and force-fed numerous times and eventually died from injuries gained when she stepped in front of King George V's horse at the Epsom Derby with the hope of bringing more attention to the cause. Emily and her fellow campaigners saw winning the vote as a vital step for women in gaining equality with men. I wonder what kind of society they imagined as they looked into the future, and what they would think of the way we live now.

Because in spite of men and women having the same rights under the law, we still experience significant inequalities in different areas of life. Nearly a hundred years after Nancy Astor became the first female MP to take her seat in the House of Commons, barely more than one-fifth of our MPs are women.[1] A recent survey of contributors to serious public debate through newspapers, radio and TV found that, again, just over a fifth of them were women. Women are in the minority in business leadership as well, and the recession has hit women the hardest with more of them losing their jobs as a result of cuts. Women still earn less than men, over 40 years after the Equal Pay Act, with those working full time earning 85p for every £1 earned by a man.

And it's not just women who are disadvantaged through inequality. Men are significantly more likely to die from cancer than women, and three-quarters of those who commit suicide are male. Men make up 95 per cent of the prison population. Girls are outperforming boys at every level of the education system, and more of them go on to higher education. There are considerably more women than men in the congregations of our churches, although the majority of church leaders are men.

Alongside these examples of inequity, many relationships between women and men are seriously damaged and damaging. Female MPs, presenters and campaigners are subjected to threats of rape and violence on social media. A 17-year-old girl who set up a feminist society at her school received an appalling and abusive backlash from the boys in her wider peer group, and her school's response was to silence the girls rather than target the boys' behaviour. Two women a week are killed at the hands of their partner, while men who suffer from domestic violence are much less likely to report it than women.

It seems that women and men are not doing life together very well.

These inequalities are damaging the quality of people's lives, harming relationships between men and women, limiting the effectiveness of businesses and institutions and restricting the freedom our children have to reach their full potential.

And yet when I read the Bible, I see a completely different vision of how things could be. God created both men and women in his image and together gave them the task of exploring and developing the world he had made as equal partners. That harmony and co-operation was disrupted when people disobeyed God, and conflict and competition entered the scene. But God always had the intention of redeeming everything that was spoilt by sin, including the distorted dynamics between women and men. Jesus related to women in a radically different way from the culture around him, treating them with respect, welcoming them into his wider community of disciples, taking time to teach them and allowing them to bear witness to his resurrection. He modelled a profoundly different form of servant leadership that didn't lord it over others or depend on hierarchy. The early Church wrestled with how to enable these restored relationships between men and women to flourish, and women took their place alongside men as leaders and teachers in the community. As followers of Jesus we are called to work out the redemption he offers in every area of life, allowing his spirit to transform our brokenness, demonstrating the wisdom of walking in God's ways and modelling something profoundly different from the damaged relationships between men and women in the rest of the world.[2]

I've also seen the liberating impact of women and men who value equality and are proactive about dismantling the barriers that stand in its way – the churches that take time to nurture all the gifts that both men and women have to offer; the parents who make it a priority to share work and the care of children so that both can pursue their calling; the households where everyone does their fair share of the domestic work; the workplaces that root out sexism and aim to open up opportunities to everyone. Equality is not just a nice concept or an interesting idea, it's foundational to women and men doing life together well. It's the environment that enables true human flourishing, where people experience life in all its fullness and pass that on to others.

But it seems to me that equality is easily misunderstood and can be a slippery concept to grasp. For a start, are men and women really equal? We're clearly different in lots of ways. We have different body parts, grow hair in different places and the difference in our chromosomes is reproduced in every cell of our bodies. In almost all sports, whether it's running, cycling, swimming or jumping, men are consistently faster than women: they jump higher, lift heavier weights, throw further and score more. That pattern of men and women achieving differently is repeated in lots of different spheres of life. How can we say that women and men are equal?

And then, aren't the differences between men and women a good thing? Wouldn't it be dull if we were all exactly the same? Where's the harm in men loving football and women preferring shopping? If women were really equal to men, wouldn't there be as many of them leading businesses, taking part in government and writing opinion pieces by now? Maybe the fact that they're still in the minority proves that actually they're just not cut out for it?

Instead of going round in circles with these types of questions, we need to explore what equality is, and what it isn't, what it means to say that women and men are equal and what stops that equality being experienced in every area of life.

## What equality is . . .

Equality is the belief that all people have the same value, regardless of any other defining characteristics such as gender, ethnicity, sexuality, disability, and age. A society or community that values equality will work to eliminate discrimination, disadvantage and barriers to opportunities so that everyone can reach their full potential. Equality is about treating people fairly without prejudice or assumptions and it's the essential foundation on which all fruitful relationships are built. Equality, particularly when we're talking about women and men, is about being free to choose the direction your life takes and having the encouragement and opportunities to enact that choice, rather than being constrained by stereotypes or cultural convention. It's about everyone being able to flourish.

I've found, in conversations about equality, that there are few people who would disagree that men and women are equal but there are lots who want to qualify that in some way. People are very quick to add a 'but' and to jump ahead to focus on difference, which is where their real interest lies. 'Of course men and women are equal but they have different roles or functions . . .' or 'but their brains are wired differently' or 'but men are natural leaders'. We'll look at difference in lots more detail later because you can't discuss equality without exploring and understanding diversity and difference, but I want to pause here and spell out in more detail the ways in which women and men are equal.

### Men and women are equally human

Again, this seems a very obvious thing to say but early thinkers taught otherwise. Aristotle said that women were a lower form of life, and Ambrose, one of the original doctors of the Church, was convinced that because Eve was created from Adam's body rather than his soul, women were not made in the image of God. Our understanding of the world and how it works has, of course,

We hold these truths to be self evident, that all men are created equal.                    *Thomas Jefferson, 1776*

An equal society protects and promotes equal, real freedom and substantive opportunity to live in the ways people value and would choose, so that everyone can flourish. An equal society recognises different people's different needs, situations and goals and removes the barriers that limit what people can do and can be.            *Leeds City Council, 2012*[3]

Equality is treating people fairly regardless of any differences between them.                    *Neil Thompson*[4]

Equality is about creating a fairer society, where everyone can participate and has the opportunity to fulfil their potential.
*Department of Health*

Equality means being afforded the same rights, dignity and freedoms as other people. These include rights to access resources, the dignity of being seen as able and the freedom to choose what to make of your life on an equal footing with others.                    *Danny Dorling*[5]

Your equality policy reflects your commitment to equal opportunities. It is your promise to treat all employees, and potential employees, fairly and considerately.        *ACAS*[6]

changed since then, but I wonder how persistent and influential this kind of thinking is and how much it has shaped current beliefs about men and women. As recently as 1993, in response to the discrimination that so many women face around the world, the UN World Conference on Human Rights found it necessary to confirm that women's rights were human rights,[7] that women are fully human. Clearly the fact that such an affirmation was required shows that the humanity of women is contested in many places, in the way they are treated if not in an articulated theory. In contrast, the creation story tells us that both women and men bear God's image: 'God created human beings in his own image, in the image of God he created them; male and female he created

5

them.'[8] Perhaps if we talked more about our common humanity and what we share as human beings made in the image of God, we would get less hung up about ways in which men and women might or ought to be distinctive.

## Women and men are equal in value

In many cultures around the world, men are valued more highly than women; they are given better food, priority access to medical care and even a greater opportunity to live. Amartya Sen was the first person to use the term 'missing women' to describe the large number of women who are not alive due to discrimination and inequality. Studies of the ratio of men to women in different countries suggest that there are an estimated 100 million missing women worldwide, 50 million of them in India, where in some communities there are as few as 85 women to every 100 men.[9] In the West, the undervaluing of women is demonstrated in the persistent pay gap between men and women. In spite of the Equal Pay Act being passed over 40 years ago, women in full-time work take home 85p for every £1 that a man takes home. In some sectors the disparity is even greater, with the pay gap rising to 33 per cent in the City of London and 55 per cent in the finance sector.[10] Surely it goes without saying that what you're paid and whether you live should not be based on what sex you are.

## Men and women have equal rights

After the Second World War, the United Nations adopted the Universal Declaration of Human Rights in 1948, the first global expression of the rights to which all human beings are entitled. Countries around the world have ratified this or related declarations of rights and integrated them into their own legal systems as a recognition of the protected opportunities that people should have simply because they are human. It sounds a simple idea, but the outworking of it is often controversial as communities try to negotiate conflicting rights and accompanying responsibilities. In 2013, the Conservatives were talking about repealing the Human Rights Act largely in protest at the obligation it imposes to pay attention to the rights of certain immigrants and offenders. It's easy to be blasé about rights when you're in a place where you can take them for granted, but in all countries they are an important route to justice and equality. The UN Convention on the Elimination of all forms of Discrimination Against Women (CEDAW), adopted in 1979, is a further attempt to affirm and secure the rights of women around the world.

## Women and men are equally intelligent

The Victorians believed that women were intellectually inferior to men, a belief that excluded women from studying at university and voting in elections. The belief in essential differences between men and women was so strong at that time that since then, from the 1890s onwards, there has been sustained empirical research to discover what those differences were and where they came from.[11] Early studies showed that actually the mental capacities of men and women were more or less equal – a fact that has been consistently upheld in subsequent studies. Very quickly at the time and ever since, everyone accepted that men and women are as intelligent as each other. It's easy to see how a belief that one group is more intellectually capable than another can become a self-fulfilling prophecy. If women are naturally less intelligent, then educating them is a waste of time; if they are not given access to education then they won't reach their full intellectual potential and will be excluded from lots of areas of life. Now, girls consistently outperform boys at every level of education from SATs to university degrees, which is a cause of significant concern. No one would suggest that boys are less intelligent; instead, people look at methods of teaching, learning and testing to see if and how they favour girls and what can be done to help boys reach their full potential.

## Men and women are equal in potential

In 1985, the Museum of Modern Art reopened in New York after a long period of renovation with an exhibition entitled 'An International Survey of Recent Painting and Sculpture'.[12] It was supposed to be a showcase of the most significant contemporary art in the world, but of the 169 artists featured only 13 were women.

In an interview, the curator of the show, Kynaston McShine, said that any artist who wasn't in the show should rethink *his* career (my emphasis). The exhibition was the catalyst for the now legendary Guerrilla Girls activists who have effectively highlighted gender and racial inequality within the art world ever since.[13] The disparity between the number of male and female contributors was, however, not really a surprise and was nothing new. Throughout history there have been far fewer women in every sphere of public life as leaders, artists, inventors, thinkers, writers, academics, theologians, priests, and the list goes on. The reasons for that are many and varied and we'll explore them in more detail later on, but while there have been fewer women in those positions they have been there in history, and they are there now; we just have to look a little harder for them.

Angela Merkel, Ellen Johnson-Sirleaf and Julia Gillard have all held the highest political office in their countries as Chancellor, President and Prime Minister respectively. Karren Brady is Vice-Chair of West Ham Football Club and a successful businesswoman. Wangari Maathai, once described by her husband as too educated, too strong, too successful, too stubborn and too hard to control, started the Green Belt movement in her native Kenya, resulting in 45 million trees being planted, and won the Nobel Peace Prize. Sheryl Sandberg is the Chief Operating Officer of Facebook. Brenda Hale was the first woman and the youngest judge to become a law lord, and is currently the only female justice of the UK Supreme Court. Aung San Suu Kyi is Burma's pro-democracy leader who has inspired the world with her resilience and determination through years of imprisonment and humiliation. Martha Lane Fox was the co-founder of lastminute.com and is a crossbench peer in the House of Lords.

Kirsty Stewart was the first female Red Arrows pilot in 2010. Alex Crawford, the *Sky News* special correspondent, was the only reporter to ride into Tripoli with the Libyan rebels in 2011 and joins Kate Adie as a celebrated war reporter. Marie Curie twice won a Nobel Prize, for physics in 1903 and for chemistry in 1911. Fabiola Gianotti is the physicist leading the biggest team working on the Large Hadron Collider. Athene Donald is professor of experimental physics at Cambridge University and is researching revolutionary treatments for Alzheimer's.

Carol Ann Duffy has been poet laureate of the UK since 2009. Hilary Mantel won the Booker Prize two years in succession for her novels about Thomas Cromwell. Franny Armstrong is the environmental activist who made the film *The Age of Stupid* and started the 10:10 campaign. Kathryn Bigelow was the first woman to win an Oscar for best director for her war film *The Hurt Locker*. Louise Bourgeois was the first artist to take on the challenge of filling the Tate Britain Turbine Hall in 2000. Zaha Hadid is an award-winning architect who has designed buildings all over the world including the London Olympics Aquatic Centre.

Olive Winchester was the first woman to be ordained in the UK, by a trinitarian church in 1912. June Osborne is the Dean of Salisbury, one of the most senior women in the Church of England; she worked as a deacon for 12 years before she was allowed to become a priest in 1994. Lynn Green became the first female General Secretary of the Baptist Union in 2013.

Hope Powell was the UK women's football team manager who took teams to two World Cups. Ellen MacArthur is the fastest person to have circumnavigated the world single-handedly. Sarah Storey and Tanni Grey-Thompson share the record for most Paralympic gold medals, with 11 each.

This is a tiny selection of women who are leaders, artists, campaigners and innovators, achieving in business, science, sport, technology, journalism and every area of life. Many of them have been pioneers who have carved their own path in spite of discrimination and barriers, which is something to celebrate. They are joined by countless unsung women who every day take initiatives, solve problems, nurture others, are resourceful, lead, challenge and serve in their families, communities and workplaces. Whether women should be allowed to do all these things is still a source of debate – which seems incredible when you read that list of names and the areas in which they have been successful – but there is no denying that women and men have the same potential to lead, create, innovate, achieve and be agents of change.

# *And what equality is not . . .*

This multi-faceted understanding of equality makes for a liberating world where women and men are free to flourish whatever their gifts, interests, circumstances or preferences and where they need to take responsibility for their own response to those opportunities. But as I've said, the issue of equality is easily misunderstood and so to add to the picture it's worth also exploring in detail what equality is not.

## Equality is not about uniformity

One of the most frequent accusations directed at those who advocate for equality between women and men is that we want everyone to be exactly the same. Traditionally, the argument goes, men and women have played different roles and exhibited different traits within society. Men have been the leaders of families and communities, the breadwinners who are rational, analytical and strong. Men are the protectors of the weak, naturally competitive and innately taciturn. Women, on the other hand, are nurturing, emotional and intuitive, inherently good at caring for others, instinctively creating community and wanting to be protected. If we blur those distinctions and encourage men to be involved and nurturing fathers, for example, or women to be ambitious and pursue leadership, then we will end up with a homogeneous mass of people who all look the same and a confusion about what it means to be a 'real' man or a 'real' woman.

But is that true? Writing about income equality, Danny Dorling says:

> Advocates of inequality . . . accuse egalitarians of being advocates of uniformity. In fact, the opposite is the case. In times and places of greater equality we are freer to each choose our individual role and how we can each contribute best. Under great inequality, the vast majority of people are condemned to lives of quite uniform poverty, while most of the rich are quite uniformly drab in their ignorance of alternatives. Under great inequality, people lose individuality by status seeking,

aping their betters and worrying more about how they are perceived. There is far more variety when we are more equal.[14]

I would argue that the same is true when we're talking about women and men. Defining a discrete set of character traits that all men or all women ought to have is extremely limiting and doesn't reflect reality. It suggests that the whole of humanity can be divided into just two distinct groups based on bodily differences, and that everyone in each of those groups will have more or less the same character traits as each other. That sounds pretty uniform to me.

Standing up for equality is not a call for men and women to be identical, but it is a call to think carefully about what any differences between women and men might mean. Rachel Held Evans, author of *A Year of Biblical Womanhood* and an advocate for equality in the USA, says: 'I believe there are differences between men and women. Some are (clearly) biological, others are (possibly) biological and still others are socially conditioned . . . I do not believe those differences to be universal, prescriptive or indicative of hierarchy.'[15] In other words, any differences that there might be between women and men don't apply to everyone, they don't tell you what people ought to be like, and they don't prove that one sex is superior in any way to the other.

We'll explore later where the differences between men and women come from and how fixed they are, but it's worth noting that you can't talk about equality without also talking about diversity and difference. True equality values and encourages difference but doesn't legislate for how it is expressed. It values the rich diversity of women and men on the planet and the different interests, gifts, personalities, talents and circumstances that they contribute to their families, communities, churches and workplaces without limiting who can do what. It recognizes that there can be more difference between two women who have had very different life experiences than there might be between a woman and a man who have been brought up in similar ways. True equality allows difference to flourish and doesn't squash individuality by saying that someone can't be like they are because of their sex.

# Equality is not necessarily about treating everyone the same

Imagine three children trying to watch a football match from outside the grounds. The oldest is just about tall enough to see over the wall; the middle one can catch glimpses of the action if she jumps as high as she can, while the youngest is so short that he can only listen to the roars of the crowd and try to guess what's going on. Looking around for a solution, he notices three wooden boxes conveniently left nearby. The oldest takes charge and insists that they share the boxes between them equally so they have one each. Standing on their boxes the two older children can now see all the action, while the youngest child, even with a box under his feet, is still left looking in frustration at the wall. After a few minutes of concentrated thinking, he comes up with another solution and persuades his older siblings to give it a go. This time, he gets two boxes, the middle child gets one and the oldest child has none. Standing on two boxes, he is finally big enough to see over the wall. Now the three children have an equal opportunity to enjoy the match, even though they haven't been treated exactly the same.

Some would argue that we live in a meritocracy where 'the cream rises to the top', where true talent and ability are always rewarded. If women do have leadership ability, the argument goes, they will end up in positions of leadership without any special help. The fact that we still have fewer female politicians proves that women just aren't cut out for politics, or perhaps aren't interested, because surely by now they can simply follow the same path into politics as men. The football spectator analogy highlights the fact that we don't all start from the same position in life. Women who want to be politicians have fewer role models, face bias from selection committees who favour male candidates, often have to juggle caring responsibilities with a pattern of work that is not at all family friendly, and need to negotiate the very male-dominated adversarial style of politics in the House of Commons.[16] Rather than trusting that eventually there will be the same number of male and female MPs in Parliament, the pursuit of equality requires us to be intentional about discerning and removing the barriers that stop women entering and progressing in the world of politics. It will mean treating women who want to be politicians differently from men in order to give them an equal opportunity of being an MP. But it will also mean recognizing the diversity among those women – that individuals will need different kinds of help – and acknowledging that there will be types of men who need barriers removing too.

## Equality won't always result in identical outcomes

There was a time when people thought that women would, with enough training, run faster marathon times than men because of the different way that we store fat on our bodies. That was until it was realized that elite marathon runners have very little excess body fat, so women didn't have any advantage after all. If you look at the world records for 100 metres, 5 kilometres and the marathon, the best times achieved by men are between 9 and 11 per cent faster than the best times achieved by women. This is unlikely to change, although in ultrarunning[17] women compete in the same races as men, over very long distances, and do well. Women's sport suffers from a lack of investment, a lack of profile and a lack of facilities across the board, but even if those issues are addressed women will never be as fast as men in the standard events.

That doesn't mean, though, that women don't show the utmost dedication and commitment to training, make extreme sacrifices to pursue their goals or invest blood, sweat and tears into being the best athletes they can be. Watching women like Jessica Ennis, Laura Trott and Shelley-Ann Fraser-Pryce at the Olympics, it was evident just how much they put into their achievements. To suggest that women's sport should not receive the same resources as men's sport or be given the same profile just because their times are slower is unjust.

## Equality isn't just about women and men

People can suffer discrimination and inequality for lots of reasons, including disability, age, ethnicity, sexuality, faith and belief, pregnancy, class, as well as their sex. Often those categories interact with each other to compound inequality, so that, for example, ethnic minority women find it harder to get jobs than white women, and Pakistani and Bangladeshi women suffer the highest unemployment rates.[18] Although boys are generally under-performing at school, it is white working-class boys who are doing the worst, with boys from some ethnic minority groups achieving higher than the average.[19] The technical name for this is intersectionality – the study of the interactions of multiple systems of oppression or discrimination.

This book will only attempt to address issues of equality as they affect women and men because of their sex, but I hope that as you read you will keep in mind these other categories, and as you act you will be able to bring liberation to other groups as well.

---

### An exercise to get you thinking

In your experience, which of these activities are typically masculine and which are typically feminine? Are there some that both men and women do equally? Divide them into three categories – mainly men, mainly women, and both. Invite someone else to do this exercise and discuss your responses together.

- Being a leader with authority
- Being an advocate for small children
- Making plans to celebrate an occasion with friends
- Crying in public
- Taking action as a result of anger
- Caring for the sick
- Teaching in church
- Spending quality time with friends of own sex
- Rescuing someone from a hostile situation
- Being a peacemaker in an aggressive situation
- Asking for help
- Making sure relatives are cared for as they get old
- Being a public figure with a following
- Taking risks
- Cooking breakfast
- Confronting people for hypocrisy

# 2

## *What are little girls and boys made of?*

On the crowded shelves of WH Smith, two magazines for runners sit side by side. *Men's Running* has advice for men on how to run to work, how to get more powerful legs, and the pros and cons of running barefoot. *Women's Running* tells women how to get marathon-ready, which so-called healthy foods will make them fat and where the best urban trails are in Britain. But are men and women really so different that they need separate magazines on how to run? And if they are, where do those differences come from? Are they there from birth or do we create them by the way we treat our children? And just how different are we anyway? John Gray suggests that men and women are so different that we might as well come from different planets, which is why we struggle to understand each other.[1] Is that true?

I think it's really important to explore these questions, because the answers we find will determine how we approach issues of equality. If there are easily defined differences between all men and all women that are down to the way we were created, then we need to live with some of the inequalities I've high-lighted and learn how to manage them better. If many of the differences between women and men are caused by the way we are brought up and the values of the culture around us, then there is more potential for us to do things differently and to think about what kind of men and what kind of women we want to be.

There's a huge amount written about men and women, how we differ, how we relate, how we're similar, how we interact, and there are lots of different opinions around. As we'll see, there's a big disconnect between popular narratives about how men and women differ and why, and the empirical evidence from research. Judith Lorber, a sociologist, maintains that when it comes to studying women and men, 'we end up finding what we looked for – we see what we believe'.[2]

With that in mind, this chapter explores current thinking about gender. I want to look at where differences between men and women come from, how significant they are, and whether we could do things differently.

## What are we talking about?

Let's start with some definitions.

The word 'sex' refers to the biological and physiological characteristics that define men and women. When you ask what sex a child is, you want to know whether they are male or female, a boy or a girl, based on what their bodies are like.

The word 'gender' refers to the socially constructed roles, behaviours, activities and attributes that a given society considers appropriate for men and women. We say that a behaviour is masculine if it's something that is most closely associated with men, such as going to watch a football match. We say that something is feminine if it's something that mainly women do, such as plucking one's eyebrows or shaving one's legs.[3] Sex is a biological category, gender is a historical or social category, although the words are often used interchangeably. Gender is often thought of as something that is only relevant to women, but both men and women have gender.

Clearly men and women differ physically; our bodies are different from each other.[4] Overall men are taller, heavier, faster and hairier, although there is, of course, a wide variety of body shapes and sizes among both women and men. The discovery of DNA has given more insight into just how different men and women are from each other. Human beings have 23 pairs of chromosomes; men and women have 22 of those pairs in common and one pair that is different. Women have two X chromosomes in that pair and men have one X and one Y. It's thought that out of the tens of thousands of genes that we have in common, we have fewer than 100 genes that are different. Several years ago, BBC News online invited readers to suggest what those genes might be. These were among the responses.

Women suggested:

- Women have the 'Oh dear, the toilet paper is on its last sheet; must replace it immediately' gene. This is entirely absent in men who have the 'Oh dear! Can you pass me a toilet roll, love?' gene.
- Men can balance an infinite amount of rubbish in the bin, without noticing it is full.
- Men have an anorak gene, which triggers a lecture on thermo-dynamics when asked a simple question requiring a yes or no answer.
- Women can smell old trainers at 100 feet; men have to hold them to their nose.

Men suggested:

- For men, 2 a.m. is time for sleep. For women, 2 a.m. is time for a discussion about where our relationship is going.
- When men want something they ask for it. When women want something they make a point distantly related to the subject and wait for a response.
- Men need a round of applause for emptying the dishwasher. Women think E on the petrol gauge means enough.
- Women have a gene that enables them to remember every outfit they have worn for the past two decades. Men can't remember what they wore yesterday without looking at the floor next to the bed.[5]

Those responses show the tendency we have to connect our gender to our sex, to assume that because men have the same bodies as each other they will also all share the same character traits, or ought to. It assumes a direct link between the ways that men and women behave and their physical bodies. But is that a correct assumption, and if so, how close is that link?

## Gender – created or constructed?[6]

The big debate around gender centres on how much of the differences between men and women are down to nature and how much to nurture. Are they essential, part of the way that God created us, and therefore intended to be universal and unchanging? Or are they constructed by the environments in which we grow up and the way we are treated from birth, with the potential for gender to change across cultures and generations and for it to be constructed differently?

### Nature?

Some people say that our gender is part of our nature, the way we were created. They see the body like a machine that produces gender differences. The reproductive differences in our bodies are mirrored in a range of other differences between men and women; one writer on gender, R. W. Connell, lists these as including strength and speed, physical skills, sexual desire, recreational interests, character and intellect.[7] Men are stronger and faster, have better spatial awareness, more powerful sexual urges, love sport, are aggressive, taciturn, rational and analytical. Women, on the other hand, are weaker, better at fiddly work, less easily aroused, love gossiping and are nurturing, talkative, emotional and intuitive. Whether you like those sets of words or not will probably depend on whether you fit the description of your sex.

More recently these differences have been linked to our brains. Simon Baron-Cohen is a professor at Cambridge and the director of the university Autism Research Centre. In his book *The Essential Difference* he argues that male brains are hard-wired for organizing and analysing systems while female brains are hard-wired for empathy. Expressed crudely, these differences are demonstrated in women getting together to chat about how they feel while men play with their gadgets and put their CDs into alphabetical order. He is careful to say that not all men have male brains and not all women have female brains, but overall there is a connection between your sex and the type of brain you have. He suggests that autism is an extreme form of the male brain, and argues that:

People with the female brain make the most wonderful counsellors, primary school teachers, nurses, carers, therapists, social workers, mediators, group facilitators or personnel staff. People with the male brain make the most wonderful scientists, engineers, mechanics, technicians, musicians, architects, plumbers, taxonomists, catalogists, bankers, toolmakers programmers or even lawyers.[8]

Christians have also written on this subject, claiming that differences between men and women are God-given and not to be tampered with. John and Stasi Eldredge's books have the Ronseal-style titles of *Wild at Heart* and *Captivating* that draw heavily on John Gray's work; they argue that men and women hunger after different roles in a fairy tale. Every man wants a battle to fight, an adventure to live and a beauty to rescue. Every woman wants to be romanced, to play an irreplaceable role in a great adventure and to unveil beauty.

## Nurture?

Others would argue that our gender identity is shaped by our experiences in childhood: that it's down to the way that we are nurtured. Studies have shown that from birth girls and boys are treated differently even by parents who try to be intentional about treating their children the same. Girl babies are cuddled more, talked to more and talked to differently. Boy babies are left to cry longer, put down on the floor earlier and held upright on their feet at a younger age.[9] Girls learn that they get affirmed for what they look like, and that they're expected to be compliant, passive and to take care of others; boys learn that they get approval when they are physical, but that playing with dolls gets them strange looks, and that 'big boys don't cry'. Girls and boys are targeted differently by advertisers and toy manufacturers, with little girls inducted into a pink princess culture and boys welcomed into a world of cars, trucks, pirates and adventure. All of this teaches children what is appropriate behaviour for their sex, and because they are so keen to please their parents and to fit in with their peers, they usually conform to gender norms and ostracize those who don't.

Simone de Beauvoir summed up this understanding of how gender identity is formed with her well-known phrase, 'One is not born but rather becomes a woman.'[10] Judith Butler is a gender theorist who argues that gender is completely constructed and is performed, not in the sense of playing a conscious role, like an actor would, but rather that we become what we do. She talks about the process of 'girling'; from the moment a female child is born and the announcement is made that 'It's a girl!', the words that are used, the actions that are undertaken and the expectations of parents, teachers, family and society all combine in the process of constructing a girl.

There are brain experts on this side of the debate too. Lise Eliot is a neuroscientist who argues in her book *Pink Brain, Blue Brain* that infant brains are so malleable that what begin as small differences at birth become amplified over time as the people who interact with those children unwittingly reinforce gender stereotypes. She says that while genes and hormones play a role in creating boy–girl differences, social factors such as how we talk to boys and girls, whether or not we encourage them to be physically adventurous and their interactions with their peers have a more powerful impact on brain development than previously realized.[11] Cordelia Fine, also a neuroscientist, covers similar ground in *Delusions of Gender*, exploring the extent to which men and women are made rather than born into predestined gendered behaviours.[12]

## A complex mix?

The debate over nature or nurture will no doubt continue, and my opinion is that gender is a mysterious and complex mixture of the two. Our gender can't be completely due to nature or the way we are created because of the diversity that we see among men and among women even within a discrete culture, let alone more significantly across different cultures in any one country, and then in an increasing diversity around the world. It's just not true to say that all men are aggressive and all women are talkative, and it's very restricting to say that they *ought* to be those things.

As for the nurture debate, it's clear that some, and perhaps many, aspects of gender are constructed by the environment in which we're brought up and our early interactions with other people. It's a complex process in which we're not completely passive, but an accumulation of these types of interactions creates an expectation within us of what's normal for a boy or a girl, and a restricted set of activities, clothes, behaviours and ways of expressing ourselves that are considered acceptable for each sex. However, even young children are active agents within that field, choosing sometimes to comply with gender norms and at other times to resist them.

At the same time we are people with bodies; our lived experience is mediated through our physical selves. Men and women experience different levels of hormones at different stages of their lives; women bleed each month while men grow hair on their faces. These physical attributes interact with our experience of the world and of being male and female. Our bodies are affected by social processes as well. For example, the age that puberty starts is lowering for girls, with one in eight now starting their periods at primary school; this is probably down to the better nutrition that we enjoy compared to previous generations.

## Negotiating gender

The study of gender shows up its complexity and sometimes leaves us with more questions than answers. Whatever the balance between nature and nurture, I think there's a lot that is known about gender that we need to pay attention to if we want to address inequality between women and men.

### We're not really that different after all

In the last chapter, I explained how the Victorians believed that women were intellectually inferior to men and how early research showed that this belief just was not true.

The interesting thing is that this conclusion of 'very little difference' is actually repeated over and over again in different areas of sex difference research. Researchers have compared large numbers of studies done in various places and times and the overwhelming conclusion is that men and women are not very different at all. Study after study, on trait after trait, comparing women's scores with men's and boys' with girls', finds no significant difference overall. Of course there will be differences between individuals, but looking at men as a whole and women as a whole, there is no difference in self-esteem, in general verbal ability, in suggestibility, in reading achievement, and so on.[13]

Connell, a leading gender theorist, says: 'We get a picture of sex differences and similarities not as fixed age-old constants of the species but as the varying products of the active responses people make to a complex and changing world.'[14] In other words, in different cultures there will be differences in the roles that men and women play, in the value that they have, in what they are allowed to do, in what is seen as masculine and feminine, in what they are encouraged to do and in the opportunities they are given, but that's not because there are easily defined God-given differences between all men and all women across the whole world. While we can make generalizations about what men are like and what women are like that are sometimes helpful, those generalizations don't tell us the whole truth.

So it's amazing that the belief in character dichotomy, in absolute gender differences that need to be protected, is so enduring and so widespread. The Victorians quickly accepted that women were as intelligent as men, but it would seem that every other finding of similarity has been resisted. Why is that?

One reason is that some small differences between genders have been found – the brain differences that Baron-Cohen and others have identified, and in visual-spatial ability, in mathematics and in aggressiveness.[15] But it's these differences that are emphasized and that make good soundbites and media stories.

But we also need to recognize the power of myths in our culture, the stories we tell about ourselves, the way we are and the way we think we ought to be. Deborah Cameron is a professor of language and communication at Oxford. In her book *The Myth of Mars and Venus* she says:

The idea that men and women differ fundamentally in the way they use language to communicate is a myth in the everyday sense of the word: a widespread but false belief. But it is also a myth in the sense of being a story that people tell in order to explain who they are, where they have come from and why they live as they do. Whether or not they are 'true' in any historical or scientific sense, such stories have consequences in the real world. They shape our beliefs and so influence our actions. The myth of Mars and Venus is no exception to that rule.[16]

So why do these myths have such resonance if there is little evidence to back them up? Cameron argues that we typically pay most attention to things that match our expectations while failing to remember or register counter-examples. Her dad, like mine, firmly believed that women were terrible drivers, so whenever they were out in the car he would point out with glee all the mistakes that female drivers were making. As you can imagine, this annoyed his teenage daughter. When, in return, Cameron pointed out good female drivers he was genuinely surprised to see them, not having noticed them before; when she pointed out bad male drivers, he would always maintain that they were an exception to the rule – that they were yobbos or Sunday drivers. When we hear that 'women talk more than men', we think of stereotypes of gossiping or nagging women and think 'oh yeah!' We forget the real people we know – both men and women – who don't conform.

Cameron then goes on to show that the proposition that men and women differ fundamentally in the way that they use language – so much so that we struggle to understand each other – is not substantiated by evidence found in research. Specifically there is no evidence that women talk more than men or that they are more verbally skilled; that men talk in order to get things done while women talk in order to build relationships; that men use language competitively while women use it co-operatively.

What she does argue is that our use of language is affected by the power that we hold in certain situations. So in those business contexts, for example, where men outnumber women and have a higher status, men will talk more and interrupt more, while women will talk more in situations where they are in the majority or where they hold the cultural power. I wonder if that's true in your experience?

Where there are differences in the way men and women communicate, we need to ask whether that is because of innate, natural differences that God created us with – in which case we'll all experience exactly the same problems across the globe in all different cultures and we're stuck with them – or is it because of the cultural context in which we live and particularly the way that power is distributed within it – in which case there is hope for better communication and co-operation?

And after all, isn't the Genesis story about the similarity between men and women as well as the difference? The first thing in God's creation that was not good was the fact that the man was on his own. Adam is given the task of naming the animals but ends up with the profoundly lonely realization that he's on his own; there's no one to help him. So God creates a woman, made from his own flesh, to be his counterpart. Adam's response when he sees her is not, 'What on earth is that alien from another planet?' but rather the poetic, 'This is now bone of my bones and flesh of my flesh.'[17] Here's someone who is just like me.

## It's more accurate to talk about masculinities in the plural than promoting a 'true' masculinity

A few years ago, James May was on a mission to remake modern man, or perhaps more accurately, to return British men to the era when they were good at making things, mending things, and generally being useful. His contention was that in the space of one generation man had been reduced to a 'feckless, bed-wetting, parmesan-shaving imbecile who revels in his own uselessness' (his words, not mine). But fear not! His *Man Lab* would show men how to do manly things such as scoring penalties, felling trees and navigating across Dartmoor when they escape from prison. The programmes were fun, nostalgic, adventurous and, I suspect, had lots of men (and women?) rediscovering the joys of making things with their own hands. They also subscribed to the 'essential' view of gender that is so persistent in our culture – that there are some things that are fundamental to a man's nature, that all men ought to be like, and if they aren't then they are lacking in true manliness.

However, the fact that James May felt a need to exhort men to rediscover their true manliness only underlines how understandings of what it is to be a man change over time. Movements like these to re-establish 'true femininity' or 'real masculinity' are themselves clear evidence that the boundaries they defend are not very stable. What studies have found in fact is that there are lots of different ways of being masculine that intersect with ethnicity, class, educational ability and so on. This idea has been around since the early 1980s and has since been studied and developed by many people. Mairtin Mac an Ghaill's 1994 study of boys, for example, discovered four distinct ways of 'doing boy' in the same school.[18]

- *The Macho Lads* were a group of friends with working-class backgrounds who thought that school work was 'girls' work', and looked down on those who stuck to the rules.
- *Real Englishmen* came from middle-class backgrounds and felt that they had better attitudes to women. They looked down on the Macho Lads, and a typical comment was: 'They all go round thinking they're real men – we're the real men.'
- *Academic Achievers* came from skilled working-class backgrounds. They were ridiculed by others for doing 'girls' subjects' at school, but emphasized that they valued intellect over emotion, which was seen as feminine. They looked down on the Macho Lads, calling them dickheads.
- *New Enterprisers* colonized the computer club and were into technology. They thought the Macho Lads gave the school a bad name.

Each group was happy with its representation of masculinity, and would defend it as being indicative of a 'real man'. They were all aware of other ways of doing or being boys and positioned themselves in relation to them. They each understood their masculinity in contrast to femininity and were at pains to point out where they were different from girls. But who is to say which one of those groups contains the 'real men'? The same is true of women, of course, although they have not been subjected to the same depth of study. It is more accurate to talk about femininities rather than trying to define what it is to be a 'real woman'.

I find this insight really liberating. People are far more complex than narrow definitions of masculinity and femininity allow – there is no 'one-size-fits-all'. When you look around at your friends, family and colleagues, you'll see a diverse mix of people with different strengths, talents, interests, personality types and ways of expressing themselves. You'll know people who don't fit the stereotypical gender norm – for example, men who stay at home and look after small children, or women who are ultra-competitive and love doing physical challenges – as well as those who do. And while there is usually a dominant form of masculinity within any culture, known as hegemonic masculinity, and men and boys in particular are very good at policing their masculinity and punishing those who don't fit the norm,[19] that diversity is enriching and to be celebrated.

We see glimmers of that diversity in the Bible as well. At times people conform to the cultural expectations of what men and women should be like, so David fights Goliath, Martha prepares food for her guests and Abraham pretends that Sarah is his sister to save his own skin – hardly godly behaviour but typical of the value afforded women in that culture. But at other times people do not fit the gender norms, with David also dancing, playing music and writing poetry, Mary learning as a disciple, Jesus welcoming children, Deborah leading a nation and Jael putting a tent-peg through Sisera's head, which is not lady-like behaviour by anyone's standards.

Men don't have to squeeze themselves into a James May-shaped mould in order to be 'real' men; women don't have to try and emulate Kirstie Allsopp's baking and general craftiness in order to be 'real' women. There can be as much difference between two women as between a man and a woman, in terms of abilities, interests, preferences, talents and so on – and that's fine. Instead of being squeezed into a mould, we can be free to be ourselves.

On the broad spectrum of gender there is space for a man whose hobby is knitting as well as a man whose hobby is boxing, and both are masculine. There is space for women who know how to replace the hard drive on their MacBook as well as women who know how to wear lipstick for more than five minutes without chewing it off, and space for women like me who can do neither, and all of us are feminine.

## We need to be aware of how our behaviour and attitudes can be affected by stereotypes

Statements like 'men are better at maths', 'women are more prone to gossip' can cause different reactions in people. Some might ignore them, or laugh them off, others may feel determined to prove the opposite and give examples of people they know who don't fit that description; others may agree with them, and perhaps think of friends who 'prove' the statement is true. But it seems that being reminded of stereotypical norms can affect our behaviour more than we realize.

Psychologist Sian Beilock recruited some female university students and asked them to take a maths test. One group of students was told that the purpose of the research was to understand why men, in general, do better than women at maths; the others were just asked to do the test. The women in the first group, who were reminded of the stereotype that women are worse at maths, did worse in the test than those in the other group, getting 10–15 per cent fewer marks. Beilock argued that they were responding to 'stereotype threat' – allowing anxiety to stop them succeeding because they knew that they were expected to fail. The same result was found with elderly people who were asked to do a memory test. Those who were reminded that memory declines with age proved more forgetful. And in tests with groups of school children, in the group that was asked to tick a box to indicate their ethnicity before completing an intellectual ability test black pupils did worse than those for whom there was no tick box.[20]

Worryingly, knowledge of stereotypes can also affect our expectations of what girls or boys might achieve. A study of primary school children by the University of Kent concluded that girls think that they are cleverer, more successful and harder working than boys from as young as four. By the time boys are seven or eight, they are in agreement and assume that girls will outperform them at school and behave better in lessons.[21] The study argued that teachers have lower expectations of boys, and that this belief fulfils itself throughout school life. Girls live up to the expectation that they will behave well and succeed academically, while boys pick up on teachers' assumptions and underperform.

As part of this study, researchers did a similar experiment to Beilock's and divided 140 children into two groups. The first were told that boys don't perform as well as girls, while the second were not given this message. Then all the children sat the same test. The boys in the first group performed 'significantly worse' than boys in the second group, while girls' performance was similar in both groups. Where there's a link between expectations and performance, it's not just teachers who are to blame. Parents, relatives, other adults and factors such as social class and ethnicity all play a part. But we need to be aware of the potential that stereotypes have to limit the expectations and achievements of ourselves and others.

## Moving on from difference

So much of the conversation about men and women focuses on defining and protecting the differences between us. Discussions about difference can be helpful if we hold them lightly and see where they fit, but they become a punishing straitjacket if we invest them with more authority than they deserve. Generalizations about what men are like or what women are like can be informative at times, but they don't tell us anything about the individual men and women with whom we interact. We need to resist using observations about the differences between men and women as an instruction manual for how to behave; rather we need to take the time to listen and to learn, to interact with the uniqueness of the real people with whom we live and work.

Often focusing on difference can be an excuse for laziness and a way of justifying immature behaviour instead of doing the work of growing up. Take just one of those statements from the BBC earlier about the ways in which men and women differ. When men want something they ask for it. When women want something they make a point distantly related to the subject and wait for a response.

Of course, not all women will identify with that statement, but some will. And for those that do, instead of accepting it as something that is universally true, that we just can't help and over which we have no control, I think we need to be asking ourselves some honest questions. Is that an honourable way to communicate with the people that we love? Why do we respect ourselves so little that we don't learn to express our opinions, our wants, and our needs? Do we really want to pass that way of communicating on to our daughters, and the young women that we know? Is that the best we can give them? Isn't it time that we grew up and took responsibility for ourselves instead of hoping that someone will do it for us and then getting angry when they don't? I know how difficult it can be to break the habits of a lifetime, but we need to do that work.

And then what can we say about those men who don't replace the empty toilet roll? Is it because it's too technically difficult for them? Is it because it's impossible to grasp what needs to happen next without an instruction manual and a few diagrams? Do men who live in all-male households have to employ someone to do it for them? I don't think so.

Does it matter if men don't change the toilet roll? In the grand scheme of things, compared to climate change, global poverty and issues like domestic violence, the answer is no. But if it's one symptom of the way in which some men assume that the women in their lives will do for them what their mums did when they were little boys – an assumption in which those women are complicit – then I think it does need some attention. And in those partnerships where both the woman and the man work, and yet the woman carries the weight of childcare, housework and the unending tasks of keeping the family running as well as doing a full-time job, then I think there's a need for those men to take responsibility for themselves. They need to begin to understand the energy that their women invest in their well-being, and the gift that that is, to try and comprehend what it's like to have domestic responsibility as the background hum of every waking moment of your day, and to start pulling their weight. Changing an empty toilet roll would be a good place to start.

As I said earlier, there is no doubt that some aspects of gender, and therefore gender differences, are constructed – by the environment in which we grow up, by the expectations of significant people in our lives and by what is valued about women and about men in the culture around us. And that means there is potential for gender to be constructed differently. We are unable to change our biology, so let's focus on what we can change and work towards a world where women and men are free to flourish whatever their gifts, interests, circumstances or preferences, and where they need to take responsibility for their own response to those opportunities.

If you did the exercise on page 14, you might be interested to know that Jesus did all of those activities in the list,[22] both those that are considered more masculine and those that are considered more feminine. Jesus is often held up as a model of the perfect man, but perhaps we need to emphasize his perfect humanity, one that everyone can learn from. In practice, all of us act in a range of ways depending on what's required of us; we are far more flexible and creative than narrow definitions of gender would suggest.

So let's go back to some of the areas of inequality I highlighted at the start of the book, and explore where they come from, what impact they have on us, and if there's any way of doing life together differently.

# 3

## *Exploring inequality*

### *Getting numbers in perspective*

At Greenbelt one year I was involved in hosting a knitting circle. We invited people to meet in a café at a designated time to knit and talk. People were encouraged to bring along their knitting but we also had patterns, needles and wool for those who didn't have any with them or wanted to learn. Around 30 people turned up, and as I expected, most of them were women. I remember there being three men – one student who brought along a scarf he was knitting, one slightly embarrassed man who had come to keep his wife company but who was willing to have a go, and one man who was knitting some intricate socks in the round and who was clearly an accomplished and habitual knitter.

If we achieve a truly equal society, where men and women are free to live life without gendered restrictions, would a future knitting circle have equal numbers of men and women voluntarily turning up? There are far more important things to campaign for than equal access to knitting but it's an interesting question because it makes us consider how we measure equality, and therefore inequality.

The measure of whether equality has been achieved is not simply numerical. The goal of progressing equality cannot only be to have equal numbers of men and women involved in a task or area of life because that measures the wrong thing. Pursuing equality is about removing the barriers that limit what people can do and can be and that needs to be where our focus lies. We create an environment where equality thrives when we are confident that we've removed all the obstacles that stop different

31

people participating in that arena. That won't necessarily result in half those people being men and half being women.

Having said that, because of the ways that I outlined earlier in which men and women are equal and because women and men are more similar than they are different, I think it is very illuminating to look at the areas of life where there are significantly more of one sex involved or affected than the other and to ask why that is. Is it a result of unequal opportunities and access, of disadvantage and damage? Does it matter that women and men are not equally represented here? What is the wider impact of there being different numbers of women and men? And do the causes of the inequality give us hints of how that could be addressed? I want to explore some of the areas of life where there is substantial numerical inequality to see what we can learn from them.

## Sport

Jessica Ennis was the face of the 2012 Olympics. Young, female and mixed race, she seemed to embody all that was good about the Olympic endeavour, and her face was everywhere in the months leading up to the event. With Lizzie Armitstead and Rebecca Adlington winning Team GB's first medals of the games and sportswomen such as Laura Trott, Nicola Adams and Jade Jones delighting the crowds with their gold-winning achievements, it was an incredible summer for women in sport, but that is not the norm.

Just eight months earlier, the shortlist for the BBC's Sports Personality of the Year 2011 was all male. In that year Chrissie Wellington won her fourth World Ironman triathlon title and broke her own world record, Keri-Anne Payne became the first person to qualify for the 2012 Olympics by winning the world 10 kilometre swimming championships, and Sarah Stevenson won her third world championship in Taekwondo, so there was no shortage of sportswomen to celebrate. Still the judges deemed Andy Murray, who was yet to win a Grand Slam title at the time, a more worthy nominee for the award.

The Women's Sport and Fitness Foundation did a study of sports reporting in national newspapers over the course of three days one March and found that 2 per cent of articles and 1.4 per cent of images were of sportswomen. There were more pictures of footballers' girlfriends on the sports pages than there were of women playing sport.[1] Overall, women's sport receives 5 per cent of media coverage and 0.5 per cent of commercial investment.[2] Often when athletes like Rebecca Adlington do get into the media, there is as much focus on her choice of shoes or nail varnish as her actual sporting achievement.[3] When they're little, girls and boys share similar levels of activity, but by the age of eight or nine girls start to do less sport than boys; by the age of 15, only half as many girls as boys take the recommended amount of exercise. There are huge inequalities between men and women in sport in terms of participation, investment and media coverage.

Does it matter? Here are just four reasons why I think this area of inequality is unhealthy and damaging.

We regularly hear about the rise in the levels of obesity in the UK, which leads to ill health, shorter lives and an increased demand on the NHS. Being physically fit and active in a way that you enjoy plays an important part in experiencing life in all its fullness and mental, physical and spiritual health. Girls say that they would rather be thin than fit, and the media promotes diets and cosmetic surgery over exercise, demonstrating the confusion that there is around how our bodies work and what we need to do to look after them well.

Second, the dominance of male sport helps to perpetuate the feelings of living in a man's world. When girls and women fail to see themselves represented on screen and in public life, they feel undervalued and excluded; their own worlds become smaller with fewer opportunities. Sport is not the only area of life where this happens, as we shall see, but it is a significant one because the inequality is so extreme. It's not enough to celebrate sportswomen every four years when the Olympics come round; we need more visibility and consistency than that. I don't completely agree with the adage 'you can't be what you can't see', because there are a great many women who have succeeded in spite of having few role models, but there is some truth in it, particularly for children and teenagers who are forming habits and attitudes that can last a lifetime.

Third, there's a complex interplay in sport between media coverage and demand, excellence and investment. Few people can reach the top of their sport without devoting themselves to it full time, which means that they need sponsorship and support. Sponsors are unlikely to invest in athletes unless they get some return in terms of profile and media coverage, in the future if not immediately. Broadcasters will only show top-level sport that they think people will watch, often because they are dependent on advertising revenue. Before the 2012 Olympics, 60 per cent of people said that they wanted to see more women's sport on TV, a proportion that rose to 75 per cent after the Games,[4] but they don't watch it at the moment because it's not there. Because of the interplay between the issues, it's no good hoping that one will be addressed and the others will follow. There needs to be a commitment to addressing the inequalities in media coverage, investment, achievement and access at the same time.

And then finally, sportswomen provide a different kind of role model for girls in an age when women are still too often celebrated for what they look like, what they wear, who they're attached to and how thin they are. Sportswomen demonstrate to all other women, but particularly girls and teenagers, that you can be strong, powerful, determined, competitive, dedicated and brilliant at what you do.

It's interesting to explore some of the reasons why these inequalities have arisen because this may give us clues to addressing them that are also relevant to other areas of life.

## A lack of diversity produces a lack of diversity

The shortlist for the BBC Sports Personality of the Year 2011 was chosen by 27 sports editors from national and regional magazines, including the 'lads' mags' *Nuts* and *Zoo*, which are not known for their egalitarian attitude towards women. Because sport is so male-dominated, most of these people were men working in a very male world.[5] I wonder if they even noticed that their suggestions included disproportionately few women. It's an unfair burden to add a couple of women to that mix and expect them to solve the problem, and it would be wrong for female contributors to suggest undeserving women, but I'm convinced that a more diverse panel would have produced a more diverse shortlist. The following year, the BBC changed its shortlisting process for the award to create a more diverse panel with more women on it; because 2012 was an Olympic year, there was no shortage of excellent female athletes who were nominated. In 2013, when Andy Murray deservedly won after his Wimbledon triumph, there were two women on the shortlist of ten – Hannah Cockcroft and Christine Ohuruogu.

## Women were banned from some sports in recent history

Around a third of the 36,000 participants in the London Marathon are female and there are more women than men in the 20 to 39 age group,[6] but the norm of women running marathons is a fairly recent phenomenon. When the Olympics were revived in 1896, a woman called Melpomene unofficially ran the marathon in around four and a half hours, although she was denied entry into the stadium and had to do her final lap round the outside. Violet Percy was the first woman to be officially timed in a marathon in 1926, and Roberta Gill sneaked into the Boston marathon in 1966, even though women were barred from entry, finishing in an unofficial time of 3 hours 21 minutes. She was inspired to run when her entry form was returned with a note to say that women were not physically capable of running that distance. Kathrine Switzer gained a place the following year by registering under her initials rather than her full name; the race director attempted to physically remove her while she was running.[7] In spite of these trail-blazing runners, the women's marathon was not added to the Olympics until 1984, just 30 years ago.

The history of women's football, currently one of the fastest growing sports, is similar. The women's game had its first golden age between the wars; over 50,000 fans turned up on Boxing Day 1920 to watch the Dick, Kerr's munitions factory women's football team, and another 10,000 or so were turned away.[8] The team had been set up to raise money for ex-servicemen and hospitals; they played all over Britain and even beat a men's team in the USA. They often drew bigger crowds than men's matches on the same day. Not everyone viewed them with enthusiasm, however, and in 1921 the FA banned the women from playing at all FA-affiliated grounds. Although this was not an outright ban, it did have the effect of sending women's football into obscurity; the ban was only lifted in 1969.

This history of exclusion has happened within the lifetime of many of the current decision-makers and opinion-formers in sport, and they leave a poisonous legacy in terms of memory, opportunity, expectations, investment and ability. Women are still playing catch-up in many areas of sport.

## Sport can harbour ingrained sexism

In January 2011, sports presenters Richard Keys and Andy Gray were recorded making disparaging comments about assistant referee, Sian Massey. Their comments were made off-air, but were subsequently passed to the media. We discovered that they thought someone had 'f***ed up big' by appointing a female match official, that she probably didn't know the offside rule and that the game had gone mad. They went on to attack Wendy Toms, the first female assistant referee in the Premier League in the 1990s, and Karren Brady, Vice-Chair of West Ham. Gray was sacked shortly afterwards, when further footage showed him making lewd suggestions to a female co-host, and Keys resigned a few days later.

More recently John Inverdale caused a storm at Wimbledon 2013 while commentating on the women's final by his remarks on winner Marion Bartoli's appearance. As she climbed into the players' box to embrace her dad, who had also been her coach he said, 'Do you think Bartoli's dad told her when she was little: "You're never going to be a looker, you'll never be a Sharapova, so you have to be scrappy and fight"?' Inverdale was publicly told that he was in the wrong, and instructed to apologize by BBC chiefs, but he was allowed to commentate on the men's final the next day. Twitter produced hundreds of extremely malicious comments about Bartoli's appearance that same day, and although Twitter trolls seldom need any encouragement to share hate, I wonder how many felt justified in holding and expressing their views because of what Inverdale had said. It's hard to say just how widespread these attitudes are but the fact that esteemed presenters and serious media channels hold them is a cause for concern.

## Women's sport lacks opportunities and investment

Nicole Cooke was the first cyclist in history to win Olympic and world road race titles in the same year. At the age of 12, after beating all the boys at the Welsh Cyclo-Cross championships, she was asked by a BBC reporter what her cycling ambitions were. She said that she would like to win the Tour de France and the Olympic Road Race. In her retirement speech in January 2013, she reflected:

> At the age of 12 one is unaware of the problems ahead. One expects there to be an infrastructure for both boys and girls to develop and demonstrate their talents; to nurture them. One does not expect that nothing is available if you are a girl or that worse still, girls will be specifically excluded, not allowed to compete. It is somewhat of a handicap trying to demonstrate just how good you are on a bike when you are not allowed to ride.[9]

She went on to explain how she and her dad fought for opportunities for her and other girls to participate on a level playing field with boys. Her dad organized races, lobbied officials, played the part of the support crew on training rides and looked for ways to get round the rules that excluded his daughter. For her part, Nicole trained hard with very little support and frequently beat older riders on more sophisticated bikes with sponsorship contracts. Arguably her success and that of others like Victoria Pendleton have paved the way for female cyclists to be taken seriously, but again, women are playing catch-up.

Until 2012 it was not possible for female cyclists to participate in as many Olympic events as men. In 2008, women had three cycling events while men had seven. Victoria Pendleton could compete for a maximum of one gold medal, while for Chris Hoy the figure was three. After a campaign for equality, the regulations were changed but parity came at a price. The International Olympic Committee agreed to increase the number of women's events only if the overall number of events stayed the same, and so in 2012 the programme of events was the same for both men and women; some events were not included, which led to Bradley Wiggins and Rebecca Romero both lodging complaints that they weren't able to defend their Olympic titles.

Bradley Wiggins, the Olympic and Tour de France champion, is a vocal supporter of women's cycling, however, and he has given high-profile backing to a new women's cycling team that has signed up the Olympic trio of Laura Trott, Dani King and Joanna Rowsell. Let's hope that the attention generated by his support and the post-Olympic window of opportunity bring more investment and opportunities for sportswomen in lots of disciplines.

## *Health*

There are many observations on difference that could be made about men and women in the field of health, but I want to pick up on a couple of areas where men are disadvantaged – cancer and suicide.

Similar numbers of men and women are diagnosed with cancer each year but because there are more women than men in the UK and because women have a longer life expectancy, there is a notable difference in incidence rates. Men are 14 per cent more likely to develop cancer and 35 per cent more likely to die from cancer than women in the UK, according to research by Cancer Research UK.[10] The difference is even starker when breast cancer and sex-specific cancers such as prostate and ovarian cancers are removed from the analysis – men are then 67 per cent more likely to die from the disease. And it's not just affecting older people, in whom cancer is more common due to age. Men under the age of 65 are 58 per cent more likely to die from cancers that affect both men and women. Cancer is the leading cause of premature death for male children and adult men and more than 40 per cent of male cancers could be prevented by lifestyle changes.

According to the Mental Health Foundation, gender plays a factor in mental health. One in four women will require treatment for depression at some point in their lives, compared with one in ten men. But it's the gender difference in suicide rates that is most dramatic: 75 per cent of people who commit suicide in the UK are men, a proportion that has stayed fairly constant for the past decade. In 2011, more men under 35 died from suicide in the UK than from road accidents, murder and HIV & AIDS combined.[11] Research by the Campaign Against Living Miserably (CALM) in 2012 found that 26 per cent of people had considered suicide 'seriously' or 'very seriously', and that was fairly equally balanced between men and women. However, three times as many men go on to take their lives.[12]

Does it matter? That seems a strange question to ask when we're talking about life and death – of course it matters that men are more likely to die from cancer or suicide when some of those deaths could be prevented. For years women have had a significantly better life expectancy than men in the western world, and while differences in life expectancy due to poverty are receiving attention, not much energy seems to be put into exploring why men die younger than women and doing something about it; it feels like it's a given. Men's lives are being cut short, and it's important to identify the reasons why and to take action.

And why have these inequalities arisen? According to the Cancer Research UK report, the reasons why men seem to be so much more prone to developing cancer than women are 'complex and still only partially understood. There may be a biological component, with women's sex-hormones and immune system being implicated in some of the differences seen, though these have not been fully explored and there may also be factors related to ethnicity and family history of cancer.'[13] However, it is possible to identify some behaviour that contributes to the relatively poor state of men's health in the UK. While we may not be able to affect the contribution of biological causes, and it's wrong to seem to blame men in any way for getting cancer or for their mental health, there is an opportunity to change behaviour and attitudes that are causing damage.

## Men can be more reluctant to visit the doctor

The 'man flu' stereotype is well established in our culture. According to this myth, men don't just have colds, they suffer from a seriously debilitating illness that women don't get, and they need lots of rest and looking after. We joke that men make a disproportionate fuss when they're ill, but evidence would suggest that men should pay far more attention than they do to illness and what is wrong with their bodies. Research shows that men are less likely to go to the doctor than women are. The Men's Health Forum found that men are 20 per cent less likely than women to seek medical help,[14] while the Gender Equity Project, which explored whether the NHS was paying proper attention to gender in its provision, found that under the age of 45, men visit their GP only half as often as women.[15] The pilot for the National Bowel Cancer Screening Programme in 2006 offered voluntary screening to almost half a million people. It achieved much lower take-up among men (52 per cent of eligible men compared to 61 per cent of eligible women).[16] The earlier cancer is caught, the more treatable it is, so any delay in getting symptoms checked out could have a serious impact.

It could be argued that women are more used to going to the doctor for routine appointments such as smear tests, or for those who have been pregnant, pre-natal and post-natal care. As most full-time parents are still women, it's reasonable to assume that they will also be responsible for taking their children to the doctor and so will be familiar with their GP and with how the system works. There can be an issue around access to doctors' appointments for people who work full time and may have to take time off to see their GP, which affects more men than women. But I would suggest that it's time to put the 'man flu' myth to death and to encourage men to take their health more seriously.

## It's culturally acceptable for women to be concerned about health issues

I often get frustrated by the way that women are constantly judged on their appearance. We grow up with the idea that it's the norm to be dissatisfied with your body and to want to change it in some way. There's a lot to critique within that cultural trend, but one thing it has given women is a greater awareness of health issues. Magazines, TV programmes and websites aimed at women frequently highlight the dangers of obesity or of not protecting your skin from the sun, both of which are risk factors for preventable cancers, and they give a context in which those issues can be discussed. Although there is much misinformation, particularly around healthy eating, at least women have available to them a constant stream of information on how to live a healthy lifestyle in an arena that many of them choose to access. Magazines like *Men's Health*, initiatives like Men's Health Awareness Month and campaigns like Movember are addressing the imbalance, but I would argue that health awareness is less likely to be on the radar of many men or in their conversations.

## Avoidable cancer risk factors affect more men than women

Around 40 per cent of men's cancer could be prevented by lifestyle changes. Although leading a healthy lifestyle is no guarantee that you will avoid cancer, it is possible to reduce the risk of contracting it. Risk factors for avoidable cancer include smoking, obesity, occupational hazards and alcohol misuse. It's interesting to see how gender interacts with those.

Similar proportions of men and women smoke,[17] but men are less likely to access programmes to help them stop.[18] When it comes to tackling obesity, lots of weight intervention programmes are female-friendly, such as Weight Watchers, which traditionally has a membership which is just 10 per cent male. It could be that men are more likely to 'go it alone' when dieting or giving up fags, but programmes such as Alcoholics Anonymous have proved the efficacy of having a supportive group to help change behaviour. Some expressions of masculinity seem to revel in an unhealthy diet and make a feature of eating lots of meat and shunning vegetables, which increases the risk of bowel cancer;[19] this was beautifully depicted in an episode of *The Simpsons*, where Homer and Bart do a conga at their barbecue singing, 'You don't make

41

friends with salad'. The incidence of people being exposed to occupational hazards that contribute to cancer such as chemicals has decreased due to certain substances being banned, but twice as many men as women contract a type of cancer that is linked to what they do for a job. The number of people being diagnosed with skin cancer is increasing rapidly and the biggest increase is in men.[20] Is that because 'real men don't use sunscreen'?[21]

## Dominant forms of masculinity do not encourage emotional intelligence

It seems that the adage 'big boys don't cry' and the stereotype of the British 'stiff upper lip' are alive and well, even in the twenty-first century. Men are not expected to show weakness or ask for help. A recent advert for McCoy's crisps, which style themselves as 'Man Crisps', shows three guys lost on a car journey, arguing over which way to go. One of them says, 'Why don't we ask someone for help?' The world goes silent while his suggestion is met by the utmost scorn, even by a dog at the nearby bus stop, and a glass column appears from the heavens and sucks him away into oblivion. It's a humorous marketing ploy rather than a sociological study, but it does tap into the stereotype of what men are supposed to be like. A campaign about mental health by the Men's Health Forum picks up on this stereotype, with posters of men saying things like 'I'd rather admit I like Justin Bieber', or 'I'd rather admit I can't get it up' than talk about 'feeling crap'.

CALM says that 'we believe that there is a cultural barrier preventing men from seeking help as they are expected to be in control at all times, and failure to be seen as such equates to weakness and a loss of masculinity'. Research by the Samaritans among older men found that emotional illiteracy – the inability to understand and express emotions and to empathize with others – was a contributing factor to high suicide rates.[22] More than half of contacts with the Samaritans are made by men – 53 per cent compared with 43 per cent by women,[23] which suggests that men are more likely to admit they need help where the stigma of doing so is removed through anonymity. But where some of the obstacles to men talking about their feelings and seeking help are addressed, quite dramatic improvements have been observed. CALM launched its first CALMzone in Merseyside in 2000. Supported by the NHS, they established a strong presence at relevant festivals and events, and built relationships with local nightclubs. Aimed at men between the ages of 15 and 35, a helpline and website are promoted through club flyers, beermats, gigs and the media, encouraging young men to open up and sort out their problems. Between 2000 and 2009, there has been a 55 per cent reduction in young male suicides in Merseyside.[24]

## Stereotypes of men may stop them getting the treatment they need

Earlier I noted that more women will need treatment for depression in their lifetime than men, but the Mental Health Foundation has found that doctors are more likely to treat depression in women than in men even when they present with identical symptoms.[25] CALM highlights the story of Nelson Pratt, a professional snowboarder who seemed to have his whole life mapped out, but who committed suicide in the summer of 2012. He went to his GP because he was feeling down, but was just given a questionnaire and told to come back in a fortnight if he wasn't feeling any better. The next day he took his life.[26] It's not possible to draw universal conclusions from that one story, and we don't know what other contributing factors there may have been. GPs have a very difficult job to do and are under immense pressure to see a large number of patients in a short time, but it would be tragic if the cultural expectation that men can cope meant that when they make the effort to seek help they don't get what they need.

## *Leadership and public life*

Over four weeks in June 2010, staff at *The Guardian* did an audit of the bylines in seven national newspapers and the reporters and guests on Radio 4's *Today* programme, and examined a whole year of contributors to BBC's *Question Time* on TV and *Any Questions* on the radio. It was a way of analysing the proportion of men and women that contribute to public discourse in the UK. They discovered that if that month and year are typical then 78 per cent of newspaper articles are written by men, 72 per cent of *Question Time* contributors are men, 84 per cent of reporters and guests on *Today* are men and 70 per cent of contributors to *Any Questions* are men.[27]

When you look at politics, the picture is similar. In their report *Sex and Power 2013: Who Runs Britain*,[28] the Centre for Women and Democracy found that just 22 per cent of MPs, 22 per cent of peers and 17 per cent of the Cabinet are women, in spite of David Cameron's promise before the election that one-third of his cabinet would be female. The report stated:

> Britain is falling down the global league table when it comes to the representation of women in politics, as other countries move forward faster: in 2001 we were ranked 33 out of 190 countries, but by the end of 2012 we had fallen to 60th place.

Rwanda, Sweden and Afghanistan have a higher proportion of female MPs than the UK.[29]

And in business, a similarly small number of women are in positions of leadership and responsibility. In 2010, for example, women made up 12.5 per cent of the corporate boards of FTSE 100 companies;[30] 20 per cent of those companies had no women on their boards at all, and just 5 per cent of FTSE 100 executive positions were held by women. The following year, Lord Davies published his review of this disparity,[31] in which he set a voluntary target for the FTSE 100 companies for women to make up 25 per cent of their boards by 2015. Some progress has been made – it's now up to 17.3 per cent[32] – but evidence would suggest that it's slowing and that below board level things are not improving.

Does it matter? Two of the reasons I gave earlier, when discussing the lack of women in sport, are also relevant here. When girls and women fail to see themselves represented in public life, their expectations and aspirations shrink and they can feel excluded and unheard. Women in politics, business and the media provide influential role models as individuals who have opinions, achieve success and shape public life.

There is also a powerful case for diversity being good for business. Lord Davies' report *Women on Boards* is worth reading for the evidence. He says:

> Inclusive and diverse boards are more likely to be effective boards, better able to understand their customers and stake-holders and to benefit from fresh perspectives, new ideas, vigorous challenge and broad experience. This in turn leads to better decision making.

The report goes on to quote some statistics: 'Companies with more women on their boards were found to outperform their rivals with a 42% higher return in sales, 66% higher return on invested capital and 53% higher return on equity.'[33]

It has long been recognized that the people who are affected by decisions should be involved in decision-making. The phrase 'nothing about us without us is for us' has its origins in Eastern Europe, but has been appropriated by people campaigning for many different causes including disability, poverty, mental health, drug users, refugees and the rights of women. When women make up half the population surely it is common sense that they should be active participants in policies and decisions that affect all of us, let alone in those issues that are most relevant to women such as reproductive health, domestic violence and childcare. As I've already said, the first thing in the whole of creation that God thought was 'not good' was the fact that man was alone. Why then do we think that it's appropriate or even acceptable for so much of public life to be controlled by male-dominated institutions? Making wise decisions is hard in our complex world. We should all be sharing in the responsibility, not leaving it up to one half of the population.

Why is there this disparity? Catalyst, a US thinktank, has published a list of the barriers that stop women getting to board level. Top of the list is women's lack of management experience, closely followed by women's exclusion from informal networks, stereotypes about women's abilities, a lack of role models, a failure of male leadership, family responsibilities, and naivety when it comes to company politics.[34] Again, some of the causes of inequality between men and women in sport are relevant here, but I would add two more.

## People tend to appoint in their own likeness

Some years ago I was on the interview panel for a youth worker, along with the vicar of the church where the post would be based. We interviewed three people and the outstanding candidate was a woman who was articulate, experienced and clearly passionate about young people. At the end of the day, the vicar turned to me and said, 'Well, I never expected that we would appoint a woman!' In his mind the ideal candidate was just like him.

Of the various strategies for increasing the number of women or men in a particular sphere of life, one of the most controversial is quotas because of the potential, for example, for talented men to be denied positions while less able women are promoted ahead of them. Norway went down the quota route in 2008 when a law was passed requiring publicly listed companies over a certain size to appoint women to 40 per cent of their non-executive board directorships. They had tried to introduce that proportion as a voluntary target, but when that didn't bring sufficient change quickly enough it was made compulsory. This caused a lot of controversy, with even some who campaigned for more women in public life very opposed to the change. However, one of the stories that emerged was very illuminating about how appointments are often made. Marit Hoel is the founder of the Oslo-based Centre for Corporate Diversity, which helps companies find experienced non-executive female directors. In response to the growing criticism that there weren't enough talented and experienced women around, she called a press conference where she said nothing. She just showed photos of 100 senior, capable, talented women with summaries of their CVs. She said, 'The pictures said it all. Experienced women are out there in quantity. The problem, as elsewhere, is that they are literally not seen. Men have their own network.' Another female executive talked about this 'grey men's club', as it's known. 'They meet in places where only men meet. They go hunting and fishing and drinking together. People who know people are appointed. I wish the quota hadn't been necessary, but I'm a realist. It forces men to look beyond their magic inner circle.'[35]

Lord Davies found something similar in his review *Women on Boards*. According to his research, some of the biggest obstacles to women reaching the top are opaque appointment methods, with half of directors recruited through personal friendships and only 4 per cent having a formal interview. He commented that many male chairmen were not thinking outside the box when it came to the selection of candidates. Virginia Bottomley, the former Tory minister, is a headhunter who has made a point of finding senior roles for women. She says:

> individuals are inclined to look in the mirror, and appoint in their image, rather than look through the window and recognise the diversity of the work environment. A board should be an orchestra that can play a harmonious tune, not just a group of violins.[36]

In her experience, one thing that is making the older men who dominate politics and business think again is the realization that their own daughters are being disadvantaged by their practice.

## Women can be slow to take opportunities

In her book *My Own Worst Enemy*, Janet Davis tells the story of how she was asked by her Bible college professor to contribute to a series of lectures that he was leading on the book of Ruth. Although she hadn't done anything like that before, she accepted and put a lot of time into preparation so that she had something significant to say. On the day, the professor introduced her and stepped aside from the lectern so that Janet could come to the front and teach. But instead of going up to the stage and delivering the lecture she had prepared, she stayed where she was, turned round in her seat and talked to the class for only a few minutes before handing back to the professional. Afterwards she was really cross that she had sabotaged herself in that way, and went on to explore whether other women had had similar experiences, writing her book in response.[37]

In the *Guardian* article on the lack of women in public life, Katie Snape, who books guests for *Sky News* and is committed to getting more women on screen, talks about the trouble she has booking the number of women she would like. She said:

> I always have these conversations with women where I say: 'We'd love to have you on the panel', and I explain why, and they laugh, and they're very self-effacing, and they say: 'Gosh, I'm so flattered, but I just don't think I'd have anything to say.' And I've never rung up a man who has said that.[38]

Whether that reluctance is due to a lack of confidence or experience or role models or something else, women who want to see more women in public life need to be prepared to be the solution to the problem and step up into the opportunities that are offered. I often tell young women to say yes automatically when they are asked to do something, and then in between the invitation and the event to get the support and knowledge they need to deliver.

## Education

Towards the end of every August there are a couple of days when the papers are full of students celebrating their exam results, accompanied by the inevitable headlines about underperforming boys. In 2013, nearly 27 per cent of girls' GCSE entries in all subjects achieved an A or A* grade, compared to just under 20 per cent of boys' entries – a gap of 6.7 per cent. This figure is up from 3.6 per cent in 1994 when the A* was introduced.[39] In that year the A-level results showed the opposite, with boys slightly narrowing the gap at A* grade,[40] but now girls do better than boys at every academic level, and more go on to higher education. In 2010, of full-time students starting graduate courses 55 per cent were female and 45 per cent male.[41]

Does it matter? Since the Victorians settled the question by discovering that men were not more intelligent than women after all, you would expect boys and girls to achieve similar results academically. The fact that boys have done less well than girls for many years would indicate that lots of them are not achieving their full potential. And it would seem that knowledge about the gender gap in education becomes self-perpetuating. I mentioned earlier the University of Kent research that found that from a very young age girls had far higher expectations of themselves, seeing themselves as cleverer, more successful and harder working than boys, while the boys assumed that the girls would do better at school than they would, both in terms of academic achievement and acceptable behaviour.[42]

In 2008, the Department for Children, Schools and Families conducted an initiative called The Gender Agenda to 'investigate, identify and disseminate practical ideas for improving the learning, motivation, involvement and attainment of underperforming groups of boys and girls'. The initiative was a response to the concern over the past two decades about the 'gender gap' in achievement, specifically boys' underperformance when compared with girls. The final report began by highlighting the fact that some groups of boys achieve very highly at school while some girls do not, and that any strategies to tackle underperformance needed to address social class and ethnicity both of which have a bigger impact on academic achievement than gender. The results of the initiative make for very interesting reading,[43] and I think there are two things worth highlighting.

## It's more complex than it would appear

Lots of reasons have been put forward for boys doing less well at school:

- They benefit from a more competitive environment than schools provide.
- GCSE-style coursework favours girls whereas boys prefer the 'sudden-death' of exams.
- The lack of male teachers, particularly at primary school, disadvantages boys who prefer to be taught by men.
- Single-sex classes are the best way to improve the achievement of both boys and girls.
- The curriculum is not 'boy friendly' and needs to be redesigned.

In fact, in the publication *Gender and Education – Mythbusters*, the initiative addresses all these theories and shows that there is little truth in them. Boys can be competitive, but with that also goes a fear of losing, so only those who are doing well thrive in a competitive environment. Those who aren't doing so well are more likely to disengage or become disruptive. Girls do just as well in exams as boys, and their results were improving before GCSE coursework was introduced. The majority of boys and girls rate a teacher's ability and care for pupils more highly than whether they are male or female, and there is little or no evidence to suggest either that pupils do better with a teacher of the same sex as them, or that male and female teachers have very different approaches or attitudes to teaching.

Single-sex classes produce very mixed results; they haven't been shown to make much difference to boys, but in some cases have improved girls' achievement. And there is no evidence to suggest that where schools have changed their curriculum to be more appealing to boys, better results for boys have followed. Gareth Malone, a choirmaster, taught in a primary school for one term in 2010 with the intention of raising boys' achievement, particularly in English. His efforts, televised in a series called *Gareth Malone's Extraordinary School for Boys*, included camping in the school grounds, cutting down trees, and physical activities that are impossible in a normal school routine. The boys made progress over the term, but quite frankly who wouldn't, with that amount of interest, time and resources being poured into them.

It would seem that education is one of the areas where intersectionality is much more significant than sex – the interplay of factors such as ethnicity, social class, parental involvement and expectation, the nature of the school and the aspirations that it has for pupils. Under the blanket headline 'boys are underperforming' is a complex reality that needs investigating and responding to with nuance and wisdom, or we could make things worse. Dividing school children into two groups based on their sex and treating one group in one way and one in another won't address the real issues and risks disadvantaging those boys who do well, and the girls who are struggling.

# Constructions of gender contribute to underperformance

Children and teenagers usually place a high priority on 'fitting in' with their peers and what society expects of them, and this is particularly true in the area of gender. Boys and girls know what behaviour, interests and school subjects they are 'allowed' to favour and which they need to avoid in order to blend in. Both primary and secondary pupils 'police' the gendered behaviour of their peers, and punish failure to conform to traditional gender norms. Boys who don't like football get teased, and girls who don't wear the right clothes or make-up are scorned.

People often assume that in order to address the issues faced by either boys or girls you need to work with them in single-sex groups, but that's not necessarily true. In fact, activities that are aimed at one sex only can endorse stereotypical understandings of what it is to be male or female, rather than challenging them or opening them up. The DCSF report *Gender Issues in Schools* states:

> Schools which attempt to alter the curriculum to provide a 'boy-friendly' curriculum not only exacerbate gender stereotypes, but their actions have been shown to be ineffective. In playing to gender stereotypes, they reinforce the idea that only some activities and behaviours are gender appropriate, and thus limit rather than enhance pupils' engagement with the curriculum. Rather, what is required to address such attitudes is a whole school approach to challenging gender cultures, which covers the school's ethos, its teaching practices and its organisation. It's in schools where gender constructions are less accentuated that boys tend to do better – and strategies that work to reduce relational constructions of gender that are most effective in facilitating boys' achievement.[44]

Stephen Frosch and his colleagues found something similar in their study into how boys aged 11 to 16 in London schools saw themselves and how they felt about their masculinity.[45] Through a series of individual and group interviews, their understanding of what it was to be a boy and how they felt they should behave was explored. It was found that it was really important to them to maintain their difference from girls and avoid doing anything that was seen as 'girly'. The popular understanding of masculinity involved being hard, being good at sport, particularly football, being cool, not caring about school work, and being dominant. It was a very competitive way of being that led to boys policing their masculinity and punishing boys that didn't fit in; homophobia is almost an essential element of real masculinity. It was difficult for individuals to 'do boy' differently, although boys who didn't fit the dominant norm were keen to assert that they were real boys. One of the conclusions of the study for how to work effectively with boys was to question the tendency of intervention projects, such as clubs or activities for boys, to offer mainly conventional 'male' activities such as sport. These can build group solidarity, but they can also actually feed into and entrench a narrow understanding of masculinity – that real boys are hard and play football – that isn't very helpful.

Rather than endorsing gender stereotypes by splitting girls and boys up into different groups and designing activities and lessons that are supposed to favour each, it is far more effective in both formal and informal education to help pupils talk about, understand and deconstruct gender, so that they don't feel constrained to behave in certain ways and they can learn to value diversity and difference, including their own.

## And the rest . . .

There are other areas of inequality between men and women in the UK that we could explore:

- *Domestic violence* – one in four women in the UK will experience domestic violence in their lifetime, and two women a week are killed by their partner. One in three teenage girls suffers some form of sexual abuse in relationships with boyfriends, while one in four experiences physical violence such as being slapped, punched or beaten.[46] Of adult victims of domestic violence 40 per cent are men, although men are less likely to report incidents;[47] women are much more likely to be victims of multiple episodes of abuse or sexual violence.[48]

- *Criminal justice* – 95 per cent of the prison population is male,[49] although women are more likely than men to be sent to prison for non-violent offences.[50]
- *Church* – a Tearfund survey in 2007 found that 65 per cent of regular churchgoers were women,[51] while the vast majority of church leaders are men. The Church is the only institution in public life that is legally allowed to exclude women from positions of leadership.

And then, women and men have different experiences of and exposure to sexual harassment, objectification, access to flexible working, eating disorders, self-harm, custody of children post-divorce – the list goes on.

Both women and men suffer from inequalities, and I don't want to get sidetracked into an argument about who is most oppressed; it's not a competition. It's easy to feel acutely the injustice and inequality that affects your own sex and ignore or belittle the challenges faced by the opposite sex. We need to listen to each other's experiences and try to work together to address them. Equality benefits us all. None of us are free until all of us are free.

These inequalities are harming people's lives and damaging relationships. They make the worlds of business, politics and the media less effective than they could be. Surely we can do better than this. There are different and complex causes for each area of inequality; here are some common factors that I've highlighted above:

- It's clear that gender stereotyping that ascribes one set of characteristics to women and another to men, and penalizes those who are different, can be really poisonous. It stops people reaching their full potential and limits our expectations of each other. Instead of promoting stereotypes, we need to challenge them and celebrate the difference and diversity that allow people to be themselves.

- We have a tendency to reproduce in our own likeness and to repeat history, so there's a real need to be intentional about addressing gender inequalities; they won't just go away.
- We all contribute to inequality, whether consciously or not, and so we each have a responsibility to become more mature, address our own insecurities and to be part of the solution.

Do any of these inequalities stem from essential differences between men and women, from the way that God created us? It's hard to argue that God would design a world when God intended men to die younger and women to lack opportunities to use their gifts and abilities. And it is clear that so many of these damaging inequalities are products of the culture we've inherited, the values we hold and the way we treat each other; they are constructed, not created. Where we can change our behaviour and attitudes to address inequalities we have a responsibility to create relationships, families, communities, organizations and a society where everyone can flourish, whether they are female or male.

So back to my question at the start. If we create an equal society, would a future knitting circle have the same numbers of men and women voluntarily turning up? I suspect not. We can't change history and it is women who have traditionally been involved in the underappreciated crafts of knitting and sewing, passing them on from one generation to the next.[52] Knitting may well always primarily be associated with women, but I would expect that more men would be present, that they would feel no embarrassment about being there, that more would have knitted before, and that ultimately we wouldn't be counting: it would be about people getting together to do something they enjoy, and we'll know that everyone is truly free to join in if they want to.

# 4

## Addressing inequality: how can we do things differently?

What would the world look like if women and men were treated as fully equal in every sphere? If we have a vision of the healthy relationships, diverse communities and enabling places of work and worship that we want to be a part of, then we have something to aim for. We also need to know where we're starting from, to take a honest look at where we are and what could be different. And when it comes to gender, that can be more difficult than we think.

### The importance of listening to stories

Ted is the CEO of a successful business, and Betty is a member of the senior executive team. Ted and Betty were talking in the corridor of their offices one day about strategy for the company and how to tackle the significant challenges that it was facing. The phone rang in Ted's office nearby, and he said to Betty, 'Could you get that?' She went to answer the phone and when she came back they looked at each other and said, 'What just happened?' They were aware that this was more than a simple case of one person voluntarily doing something for another. Although they were peers in the company, Ted had just spoken to Betty as if she were his secretary, and she had unthinkingly complied as if that was her role. In an unguarded moment his actions revealed an assumption that a female colleague should do his bidding. Ted liked to pride himself on treating both male and female colleagues as equals, and this experience shook him; it made him realize that maybe he wasn't as enlightened as he had thought.

This story is told by Patricia Yancey Martin, who has studied gender and organizations for many years. She talks about the importance of 'catching the sayings and doings of gender',[1] becoming more aware of the ways that women and men relate to each other, particularly in our instinctive reactions and unguarded moments. It's possible to say and think all the right things about the equality of men and women, but then to act differently because patterns of behaviour and the influence of our background can be deeply ingrained. We need to take time to reflect on our actions and to listen to the experiences of others to find out how gender affects the real-time activities of our lives. We must respond to the reality of who we are and what we are like, not the stereotypes of what men and women ought to be. We can allow space for diversity to emerge through listening to people's different experiences, and for stereotypes to be questioned and, if necessary, deconstructed.

I'll give you some examples of what I mean.[2]

- Heather and Josh are intentional about sharing work, parenting and domestic life. They each have two days off a week, with just one of these being shared. On their separate days off they do very different things. Josh watches sport, reads the Sunday papers and generally chills out; Heather cleans the house, does the gardening and feels guilty if she relaxes or spends any money. Her actions show that deep down she perhaps feels that she has the responsibility for the home, or she is trying to live up to an image of what a good wife should be like.
- Amanda is a vicar in her first parish. She has been through the selection process of the Church of England and has completed a curacy where her ministry was appreciated. When, in her new role, she approached a local minister to see if their churches could work together, he told her that he couldn't work with her because she was 'in sin' as a woman in leadership. She left the meeting quite shaken, questioning whether she was doing the right thing, even though she was good at her job and many others had confirmed that this was what she was called to. The knowledge that others oppose who you are and

what you do can be surprisingly undermining for many women in leadership.

- A few years ago, I read the story of Bluebeard and was shocked by my reaction to it. In summary, Bluebeard seduces a young woman and takes her to be his wife. One day he goes out hunting and gives her the keys to his castle. He tells her that she can go into any room except for the one that is opened by the smallest key. The woman and her sisters set off to explore and eventually they come to the last door in the castle, the one that is opened by the smallest key. They open it, and inside the room they find the bodies of Bluebeard's former wives. They lock the door again, fearful of Bluebeard's return, but the key starts weeping blood, threatening to give them away. My gut reaction to that story was, 'She should have done what she was told.' Effectively I was saying that she should have ignored her instinct to investigate, that she should have obeyed her murderous husband even though that put her life at risk. I was brought up in the Brethren Church to be a good girl who keeps people happy, and although I've been an advocate for the equality of women and men for over 25 years, and shared both work and parenting for most of that time, my response revealed just how deeply embedded those childhood values are.

Getting conversations going to catch the sayings and doings of gender can be tricky. For a start, many people misunderstand the word 'gender' or think it's synonymous with women. Virginia Luckett works for Tearfund. At a time when Tearfund was conducting a gender audit she took part in a conversation about gender in her team. She says:

> Initially the male leaders went on the defensive because they thought it was all about women. I encouraged them to think about family policies and aspects of Tearfund's working practice that impacted them as fathers and as men. That was it! Then they got talking!

Women have been talking about their experiences of being women for years; men may need time to catch up. Michael Kimmel, a sociology professor in New York and an advocate for the equality of women and men, says that in his experience not many men are aware of gender and how it affects them. He says, 'When I wake up and look in the mirror I see a human being – the generic person. As a middle-class white man, I have no class, no race and no gender. I am universally generalizable. I am every-man.'[3] Some men may need different routes in to talking about gender issues, as Virginia Luckett found. Here are some questions you could use to get conversations going. Invite people to talk about themselves and their own experiences first, rather than what they think life is like for the opposite sex, although that can be helpful too.

- In your experience what's the best/worst thing about being a man/woman?
- When have you felt that it's an advantage to be a woman/man? When have you felt that it's a disadvantage?
- What would you like to change in society's expectations of men/women?
- Where do you experience inequality as a woman/man?
- Do you feel under pressure to be a certain type of man/woman? How do you feel you are different from that norm?

It can be liberating to talk about our experiences of being men and women and to be heard and understood. It's important to name injustice and discrimination for what it is, and to recognize that we don't have to put up with oppression or sexism. It's encouraging to realize that there are other people who feel the same way and that we can take action together. However, it is also possible to have a good whinge, or to rehearse stories of injustice and hurt so often that they get embedded in us instead of being something that we can move on from. Let's aim for a balance between the two.

Once we have a sense of where we are, and where we want to get to, it's time to bridge that gap. As I've said throughout this book, we need to be intentional about dismantling the barriers to equality if we want a more equal world; it won't just happen.

## Taking action

There are many ways of taking action to bring about change. Sometimes small changes to the way we live can have a big impact; at other times it needs more of a concerted effort and an organized campaign with lots of people on board. Sometimes we can only change ourselves, but that can ripple out to have more of an influence than we thought. We can take action as individuals, as groups and as organi~~~~~~~~ ~r institutions to enable equality to ~~~~~~~~~~ les of what people have done.

### one person

 change ourselves, the tendencies in the man changes his own nature, so change towards him . . . We need ' This is often summarized as 'Be nge needs to begin with ourselves, ons and in our relationships with others with equality and respect, cross sexism or the exclusion of r share of the work involved in 't underestimate the impact this

and sees first hand the effect that ~~~~~~~~~~~ of girls has on the young people she works with. On her way to work one day she passed a bar with a poster advertising a wet T-shirt competition, which clearly showed a girl's nipple through her wet shirt. Ruth says, 'I am not nipplephobic; I have two of my own. I object, though, to having to see other people's as I go about my day-to-day life.' She decided to do something about it. She wrote on a sticker the words 'Women are not objects', and placed it over the nipple. She rang the local council to try to get the poster removed, and was passed between four departments before being told that there was nothing anyone could do as the poster was on private property. She rang the Advertising Standards Agency, and contacted the police, who gave her an incident number to keep her happy. She then sent some emails: to her local councillor to complain that there seemed to be no regulation of local advertising, to her local newspaper, and to the bar itself with her concerns. On her way home she saw that the poster was gone. Later she got an email from the bar manager, who apologized, saying that the poster was not normally put up until 9 p.m. and it had been displayed as a mistake. Reflecting on her action she says, 'With a bit of perseverance I can bring a little bit of change.'[5]

## Collective action taken by a group of people

In the summer of 2013, the Bank of England announced that in 2016 they were going to bring out a new £5 note, on which the image of Elizabeth Fry would be replaced by one of Winston Churchill. This redesign would have meant that there would only be men represented on English banknotes. Caroline Criado-Perez, a journalist and activist, started a petition calling for the Bank of England to keep women on banknotes. The petition attracted over 36,000 signatures and was delivered to the bank by a group of women dressed up as key female historical figures. Mark Carney, the new governor of the Bank of England, met with campaigners in his first week in the role. The outcome was that when the new £10 note comes out in 2017 it will feature Jane Austen, and the bank has reviewed the way it makes these kinds of decisions. Although some people dismissed the campaign as trivial, it generated a huge amount of interest and resulted in public discussions about the sidelining of women in history. It also unearthed some appalling misogyny; Criado-Perez and others were subjected to vicious rape and death threats on Twitter because of the campaign.

## Action taken by an organization or institution

I belong to a creative worship community in Ealing called Grace. We like to think of ourselves as egalitarian, and encourage participation by as many people as possible. A few years ago we realized that we had got stuck in very traditional roles. The men had all the gadgets for use in worship; the women ran the café after the service. We acknowledged that these were our comfort zones, and where our skills currently lay, but it was not necessarily a healthy place in which to remain. We deliberately tried to learn new skills, to encourage each other to participate in all types of activities and to strive for balance in the roles we play within the community. In doing so, we opened up new possibilities. When Dean Ayres took a turn at doing the café he came up with a new way of organizing it that minimized the distinction between hosts and guests and enabled more of us to get to know those who were visiting. We had to acknowledge that there's a difference between being called to and gifted for a particular role or position, and sticking with roles through laziness or comfort.

Sometimes these three types of actions will intersect with a fourth: legislative change, where the type of community that we collectively want to be is enshrined in law so that it can be enforced. The Equalities Act in 2010 brought together over 100 pieces of legislation that cover all types of equality, to protect people from discrimination in the workplace and in wider society, and goes some way to signalling that equality is an important value in our common life.

Both men and women can take action in lots of different ways to address inequality, and if they do it together that's even better. The remaining chapters of this book explore how barriers to equality can be dismantled in various areas of life, but I'd like to start with some foundational ways in which both men and women can create a more equal world for each other.

## Lay down power

One of the few places where the Bible uses the word 'equality' is in Philippians 2.6: Jesus, although he was God, 'did not consider equality with God something to be used to his own advantage; rather, he made himself nothing by taking the very nature of a servant'. At the Last Supper, John tells us that Jesus knew that the Father had put all things under his power, that he had come from God and was returning to God and so he chose to serve.[6] Jesus invites us to follow his example, not grasping for or holding on to power but to be secure enough in our identity in Christ to lay it down so that we can serve and others can shine.

For some women, but by no means all, this will mean laying down power in the home. My friend Alison[7] has three children, works part time and juggles a number of responsibilities, as she chooses to do all the domestic work involved in running the household. Her husband is intelligent, competent and confident but is not a great cook. If she wants to go away for the weekend she makes elaborate arrangements for either her mother or mother-in-law to come and stay with her husband and children, or else she leaves prepared meals and copious instructions for him so that he can manage on his own. She doesn't go away very often. I ask her why she and her husband don't share the domestic work, or why he doesn't cook from time to time. She laughs and says, 'If he cooked, we'd have burnt pizza every week.' The truth, as she would admit, is that she likes to be in control and prefers things to be done exactly how she wants them, which is not the way her husband would do them. It's not that he's incapable, or even unwilling, it's that she won't let him have a go.

In her book *Shattered*, Rebecca Asher argues that women's hopes for equality are disrupted by the arrival of children, but sometimes we have only ourselves to blame. She says:

> in reaction to our loss of social and domestic status outside the home, we grip the reins in our domestic life ever more tightly. We collude in distancing the father from the domestic sphere. The home becomes our domain, our power base. We decide that we will exercise control there if nowhere else.[8]

It seems a very self-defeating attitude, and one that denies fathers the delights of hands-on parenting. What makes women think that they have more right than their partners to be involved in their children's lives?

For some men, but by no means all, this will mean laying down power in the workplace or church, giving up opportunities that come their way so that women can take advantage of them, or being intentional about developing the skills of female colleagues even if that results in men being surpassed. Women who have fought hard for positions of influence sometimes have a tendency to hold on to them once they've achieved their goal; they too need to learn to lay down power and create opportunities for others. Let's resist the temptation to build a profile for ourselves and then to believe it. We all need to deal with our insecurities and our tendency to feel threatened. Our security must be in Christ, rather than in what we do and how people perceive us.

## Speak up for equality

Research into teenage relationships by the NSPCC and Bristol University found that a third of teenage girls were subjected to some form of sexual abuse from their boyfriends, while a quarter suffered physical violence such as being slapped, punched or beaten.[9] A small minority of boys reported having been pressurized into sexual activity and around 20 per cent had suffered physical violence from their girlfriends. On the whole, boys would end a relationship if their girlfriend hit them but girls were more likely to keep quiet about the abuse they suffered, either believing that it was normal or fearful that they would lose their boyfriends. It's alarming that so many people think that violence is an acceptable part of what should be a loving relationship, but to those girls it's part of the deal; it's their normality. And how will that change unless someone tells them that it doesn't need to be like that?

Violence in relationships is perhaps an extreme example, but it highlights how we can get so used to the context we live in that we simply accept the way things are. If we want to create an environment where equality can flourish, we have to name the obstacles that are blocking the path, and ask questions about the way things are done. We might pick someone up on their use of sexist language, query why an event has an all-male speaking team, or expand the horizons of a child by helping them to question the gender stereotypes found in books, films or toys. This needs to be done with sensitivity, of course, and no one wants to be a single-topic bore, but the fact remains that it needs to be done.

Men's voices are vital in this conversation too, and in some contexts it is only men who will be listened to. A church leader who doesn't believe that women should preach is unlikely to listen to me trying to persuade him, but will find it harder to ignore a man advocating for female voices. It can be difficult for men to know how to intervene sometimes. Writing in *The Guardian* on this issue, Jonathan Freedland says:

> Somehow men leave the heavy lifting against gender bias and gender hatred to women. The most charitable explanation is that men worry they cannot speak about this subject authentically, that their perspective is of less value than a woman's. Others fret they'll get it wrong, that they'll inadvertently say something that is itself sexist, thereby revealing that they too don't 'get it' – so it's safer to say nothing.[10]

But equality should not be labelled as a women's issue; it's important to see it as a human issue, and appreciate that inequality between men and women diminishes us all.

Steve Holmes writes on his blog about how he has struggled with whether or not to speak up. He concludes:

> I have been told many times that I moved someone to tears just by saying something simple about this or that issue of prejudice. This always takes me by surprise; if I sometimes 'get it' where 'it' is the wrongness of prejudice, I have to admit that I really do not 'get it' where 'it' is the power of prejudice to disable, disempower, dehumanise a person. And so I do not 'get it' where 'it' is the power a very simple intervention can have. I don't particularly need to understand what it feels like to be threatened with rape . . . I need to understand what it feels like to have someone – particularly perhaps someone who stands in a position of privilege – intervene, stand up and say such threats are not OK.[11]

## Do things differently

The proof of our beliefs is not in what we say, but in what we do. Although agreeing that equality is important might be the first step, nothing will change if it's the only step we take. We need to make tangible, embedded choices to do things differently. Sometimes that means doing the opposite of what's expected of your sex – so a man might choose to make cakes for a church event when only the women have been asked. Sometimes it means doing a thing for yourself instead of expecting someone else to do it for you – so a woman might learn to change the inner tube on her bike instead of taking it home to her dad. Sometimes it means deliberately modelling an attitude that makes people think – so a man might refuse to contribute to an event that has an all-male speaking team. And sometimes it means not doing what might be expected of your sex – so a woman might choose not to make coffee for colleagues at a work meeting to remind them that they should not assume that she should play that role. Often it means choosing a more difficult route in the first instance, but one that becomes easier and more natural as it goes on. These might seem like small actions when arguably we need new ways of organizing communities, institutions and the wider society that are free of their patriarchal roots, but it is better than doing nothing and can raise awareness, start conversations and have a snowball effect.

## There is no blueprint for equality

In the chapters that follow I explore in detail how we can put equality into practice in the home, marriage, parenting, at work and in the Church. In one sense these chapters will be a 'how to . . . ' guide to equality in that they give practical examples of what other people have done, things to think about and tips for addressing inequality in different areas of life. However, it's really important to understand that there is no blueprint for equality, no one-size-fits-all list of what to do to achieve it. That's particularly true the smaller the group of people involved, because that's where diversity will be more noticeable. How one household shares the domestic work equally between them will be different from how another household does it. How one couple divides up the hands-on aspects of parenting will be different from the way another couple does so. We need to take account of our various personalities, skills and preferences while also being aware of the default patterns we'll fall into if we're not paying attention.

A whole book could be written on each of these areas of life, so my suggestions will be by no means exhaustive. But I hope they spark conversations, show different possibilities and get people exploring the potential of how they could do things so they are doing life together. Not all the chapters will be relevant to everyone, so feel free to pick and choose.

# 5

## *Home life and equality*

————◦•◦————

At the start of the film *Gladiator*, Russell Crowe speaks to his soldiers as they are about to enter battle. Exhorting them to stay strong and fight well, he appeals to their sense of destiny with the words, 'What we do in life echoes in eternity.' Slightly tongue in cheek, I find myself wanting to say something similarly epic to all those fighting for a more equal world for men and women, 'What we do at home echoes in the rest of our lives.' Second-wave feminists in the 1960s coined the phrase 'the personal is political' to capture the connection between the decisions women were making about the way they ran their lives and their campaigning on bigger issues such as equal pay and human rights. If you want to see a more equal world, then it matters who cleans the toilet in your home.

### *Domestic work – fair shares*

Women no longer believe the myth that they can have it all – a fulfilling career, a perfect home, adorable children and a fantastic marriage, but many of us would like to share it all out a lot more fairly than happens at the moment. Whether you're still living with your parents, sharing a house with friends, married or living with a partner, or a single parent with children, this is why I suggest that you need to get everyone in your household contributing to the domestic work that keeps it running smoothly, in case you need convincing.

### It frees up time more equitably

Many women who are working still end up holding on to responsibility for running the home. After a day at work, they come home to do the double shift of cooking, washing, cleaning and organizing. There are all kinds of reasons for this. Some choose to do so because they like things done a certain way; some want to assuage their guilt at not being a stay-at-home mum; some genuinely want to look after their families well; some just assume that it's their responsibility; some don't want the hassle of trying to get reluctant housemates or family members involved. Whatever the reason, it means that there are a lot of exhausted women out there. Carrying the weight of responsibility for the organization of a family's life can take up a considerable amount of mental and emotional energy, as well as time. Sharing the load leads to a sharing of leisure time as well and a more balanced life for everyone. It generates time to read, study, create, dream, play and explore. And that, of course, means that some in the household will need to start doing more.

## It's an essential part of growing up

When I was a child, my mum made sure that I was fed, had ironed clothes to wear and lived in a clean, organized home. As I grew up I took on those responsibilities, with varying degrees of success. Some relationships between men and women can remain very parental, with men expecting their partners to do for them what their mums did when they were little boys, and women assuming that their partners will fulfil the role of their dads. Surely the physical aspects of looking after yourself – cooking, cleaning, washing – are a part of being an adult, and to do all that for someone else is to keep them immature and dependent, to deny them the satisfaction of growing up. Parents who don't get their teenage children involved in running the home do them a disservice because they will be less prepared for the time when they branch out on their own.

## It stops us taking each other for granted

When you're used to someone clearing up after you, it's easy for that to become so much a part of your everyday life that you barely notice it happening, and you genuinely don't see what needs to be done. When you take it in turns to cook, for example, you really appreciate the days when someone else produces the meal and it's natural to express that gratitude.

If people are used to being 'looked after' at home, there may also be an unspoken expectation that this will happen everywhere; and because women have traditionally done the housework, it can become an assumption that the women will do the looking after. If we want to create a different world then we need to subvert the status quo and demonstrate something different. Vicky says:

> In many churches I visited while working for a ministry, if we ate at pastors' houses, the wife would be in the kitchen cooking for everyone while the men sat around chatting. I would often go and help, gritting my teeth that it played into the stereotype, but disliking that a woman had to do everything and the men got to eat, tell her how well she had done and go back to talking about the real business.

In that situation, it would be great to see men helping out with the preparation or clearing away, so that everyone can join in the conversation. And men who are already contributing to the domestic work in their own homes will find that it comes naturally to do that in other settings as well.

## Putting theory into practice

Seeing the need to share the domestic work is one thing; putting it into practice is another. Each individual household will need to sort out what works for them, but here are some things to think about, along with tips from people who have tried to make it work. Many of the examples come from couples, but single people sharing households can have the same conversations.

### Decide early on and stick with it

Making a decision to share housework is obviously the first step, but it's surprising how many people don't even discuss who will do the work involved in running the home. Writing on his blog, Dave Westlake reflects on his experience of doing housework:

> A few months ago we had one of our periodic attempts at getting our home life organised. As part of this I committed to clean our bathrooms and toilets every Saturday morning. And depending on who you talk to I have managed this somewhere between quite often and occasionally. No big deal. I use the bathrooms. I clean them. The strange thing wasn't me doing some housework, it was the reaction of our female friends and acquaintances when Minu casually mentioned it. There were gasps of shock and praise and jealousy. 'You are so lucky,' they said to Minu, 'Isn't he good.' Now I am prepared to take praise whenever it comes, but 'good'? I think I am somewhere on a line between 'doing my fair share' and 'doing the bare minimum'. The shock was how many of our male friends do nothing in the home and think that is OK. A bigger shock is how many of our female friends seem to collude with this. I have one friend who has been married for 12 years and does not know how to use the washing machine. Now I am fine about couples making a pragmatic choice about dividing up the stuff that makes life work in order to get things done. My fear is that men are significantly underperforming at home based on an assumption about roles rather than intentional choice.[1]

It helps if you make this decision early on in a relationship or house-share before you get stuck in patterns of relating that you haven't necessarily chosen, but it's never too late. Sit down with the people you live with and talk about how things are working now, and how they could be different. This can be a sensitive area, of course, especially if people feel taken for granted or accused of not pulling their weight. The suggestions on pages 74–6 might help to frame the discussion and keep it healthy.

## Reach an agreement on how you'll share out the work

There are as many ways of dividing up domestic work as there are different types of family or household, but here are some things to bear in mind.

- Do you actually know how much different people are contributing at the moment? If you feel taken for granted, it can be easy to feel as if you do 'everything' and to miss what is being done by others. On the other hand, some might be surprised to find that the Sunday lunch washing-up that they do with pride hardly balances everything else that is done for them. Could you find a way for each person to record what they do over a week or a fortnight, and to use that as a starting point for discussions?
- It's important to recognize that each of us has different strengths. Bridget says: 'God has designed my husband to be good at hospitality; I find hospitality hard. God's designed me to be well organized, not a quality my husband has in abundance! I'm good at managing the family finances; he does the internet food shop. We work well together because we each play to our strengths.' Linda says: 'Before our marriage we talked about expectations around the house and home and went with the standard divide that he'd do the finances and I'd do the washing. After several months of marriage I came home one evening and he was pulling his hair out doing the preparation for filling in tax forms. He asked me what he could do instead of the finances. We swapped. I did the finances and he did the washing. It suited us perfectly.'
- You need to balance people's preferences and skills with the fact that there will be tasks that no one would choose to do. In our house it's ironing, so in practice we each do our own and iron as little as possible. Fran and Craig have devised a brilliant way of dividing up what needs to be done so that both of them do things they enjoy, but they share out the horrible jobs too; you can read about their method on pages 76–8.
- People will obviously have differing amounts of time available. If you are out at work all day housework has to be fitted into evenings or weekends; it may be tempting to leave it all to a partner who is at home more. Sometimes that is the practical solution, but you may choose to take responsibility for particular chores even though time is short. For example, Dave's commute to and from work takes four hours each day, and he

often stays overnight during the week, to cut down on travel. While he contributes generally to the housework when he can, the one task he always does is the ironing; having something that's his responsibility helps him feel that he's making a contribution even though his wife inevitably does more. As I said before, a commitment to equality doesn't mean that everything needs to be shared 50:50 because that's not always possible.

- For those bringing up children, it probably helps to make a distinction between childcare and housework. Clearly there's a lot of overlap; looking after children includes a huge amount of washing, shopping, preparing meals and so on. But just because you spend most of your time looking after children, it doesn't mean that you need to do all of that work for everyone else in the house as well.

- No one is born with the ability to cook a delicious meal; we all need to learn. Women tend to get more opportunities to learn and practise, and then it becomes a habit. Men may never have learned to cook, and because their partners do it so well they let them get on with it. (Of course in some households it's the other way round.) Choosing to share a task that you find easy with another who doesn't may become quite a painful process, watching the other person struggle with a task you could do much more quickly yourself. But it's worth persevering, not least because you can't assume that your partner will always be there.

- A decision to share housework means sharing the responsibility for getting it done. It doesn't work if one person feels that they're still in charge overall and the other person is just helping them. When Jonny cleans the kitchen floor each weekend, he's not doing it to help me out; he's contributing to the smooth running of his own home. It's a small distinction but an important one. As mentioned earlier, some women will need to relinquish their power in the home, accepting that things may be done differently and resisting the temptation to interfere.

- It might be helpful to agree acceptable standards for some tasks. Does doing the washing also include sorting the clothes once they are dry and putting them away, or does someone else do that? Does cooking a meal include washing up as you go along, or can the pots and pans be left until after the meal? And if so, who washes them up then? Does washing up include wiping down the surfaces in the kitchen or cleaning the top of the cooker? It may sound tedious but it's important to talk through expectations to make sure that you are all on the same page. It's possible that people will need to be taught how to use the washing machine, for example; don't assume that it's obvious what's required.

## Compromise and review

If the default position in your house has been that one person does most of the domestic work, then it can take a while to reset it. Once you've decided how jobs will be shared out, agree a time period to give it a go and then sit down together to review how things have gone. Everyone needs to commit to the responsibilities they've taken on, and there needs to be trust from others that everyone will do what they've said they will do.

It will be tempting for the individual who used to do most of the work to supervise or police what others are doing. Resist doing this during the trial period; don't nag, and don't step in if others aren't sticking to what they said they would do. There may be a period of relative chaos as people adapt to new ways of doing things, and inevitably some compromise will be needed over standards or methods. If you have long felt that it's your responsibility to run the home, you may feel guilty as others do the tasks you've previously done for them. I can remember suffering immense ironing guilt when I saw Jonny ironing his own shirts shortly after we were married, not because I love ironing but because my mum had always done it for my dad and somewhere deep within me I felt that's what I ought to do too. I had to sit on my hands or leave the room to stop myself taking over. Fortunately that feeling soon passed; now, if I feel anything when I see others in my house ironing it is delight that they are just getting on with it.

When everyone in a household genuinely shares in the work needed to run it, soon you will no longer notice who is doing what or keep track of how much you've contributed. When something needs doing you can just get on and do it, in the knowledge that others will do the same. The ideal is for people to treat each other with kindness and generosity, to serve one another with love, to willingly do more if one person is under stress, to surprise each other with thoughtful acts. While you're creating your new normal, it may feel as if all this has gone out of the window; don't worry, you'll get there. Persevere, keep talking to each other, make adjustments and keep the greater goal of a more equal world in your sights.

## Conversations about equality

No doubt you know from experience that conversations are not always about the thing that's being discussed. It might seem simple to sit down and talk about how to share out the housework, or any other part of life, more equally, but it's not. It's easy for one person to become self-righteous and another to feel attacked, for one person to feel taken for granted and another to feel judged or get defensive, for hidden resentments to surface or for past experiences to affect how ideas are expressed or heard. But don't let that put you off! Go through these ideas together before you start talking about the issue and decide together which are important.

### Agree the goal

Talk about why equality is important and how you want life to be different from the way it is now. Keep this bigger goal in mind as you talk through the details.

### Talk about facts

You might feel that you do everything and others in your house do nothing, but that's probably not true. Find out who does what and what each person contributes. Talk about specifics rather than generalizations.

### Own feelings

Own what you feel and think by using statements like, 'When I come into the kitchen for breakfast and your washing-up is still there from the night before, my heart sinks', instead of, 'You make me so upset when you don't do your washing-up.' Try 'I feel unappreciated' rather than 'You just take me for granted.'

### Avoid universal statements

Comments that begin 'I always . . .' or 'You never . . .' are very rarely true, even though it might feel that way, and they sound very accusing. Rather than saying, 'You never clean out the fridge', try, 'I feel like it's usually me that cleans out the fridge – is that right?'

### Be assertive

Aim to be assertive; express your point of view clearly while also respecting others. Avoid being aggressive where you're dismissive of others; don't assume that your point of view is right. Don't be passive either, not expressing an opinion at all and letting others do all the work. Make sure that you're not passive aggressive either, where any anger or frustration is not expressed openly but is clearly communicated through sighs, facial expression or body language.

### Listen and listen again

Don't assume that you know what others are thinking or feeling, or what their motives or intentions are. You only have access to your own stuff. Listen carefully to what others are saying, and ask questions to make sure you understand. Reflect back what you think has been said to check that you've heard correctly: 'It sounds like you're saying that you really don't enjoy cooking when you have to do it every night – is that right?'

### Don't be afraid of conflict

When we get into disagreements, the temptation is either to get angry and confront or to shut down and withdraw. Aim to stay in the middle; be clear about what the problem is and how you might address it. Don't rush to smooth things over too quickly. Working issues out together means that the real problems get addressed.

### Allow for people's differences

Some people are good with words and can articulate their thoughts quickly and easily; others require more time to reflect, or need to talk in order to work out what they're thinking. If you're good at talking, don't use that advantage to rush people into decisions or override what they want. If you're finding it difficult to put your thoughts into words, say so; ask for five minutes' break or offer to make a cup of tea while you think.

### Keep the conversation going

It's unlikely that you'll be able to reverse the patterns of a lifetime in one conversation. Agree what action everyone will take, and when you will get together again to talk about it some more.

## Dividing up the housework

When we first got married, the mundane domestic chores of life were new and exciting. We could not do enough for each other and took great joy and delight in our new little flat. Needless to say, it did not stay that way for ever! Resentment can set in rather quickly when one person feels that they are doing more around the house than the other, or that they get all the horrible jobs and the other all the good jobs. We needed to find a way of enabling equality in our domestic life. We both lived by the principle that equality was not everyone having the same but about each person having their needs

met to an equal extent. There were some jobs I was good
at, did not mind doing and didn't take much time. There were
also some things I hated and some things I could not do,
like driving. The same was true for Craig. We needed to find
a way that we could both be happy with our own offering to
domestic bliss and trust that the other was contributing to
the same degree.

We listed all the domestic chores we do on a two-week
basis. Even this took some discussion; what is a domestic
chore? We then both rated each task out of three, for difficulty
and for how time-consuming it was. There's a section of that
list in Table 1.

**Table 1 Rating of domestic tasks**

| Job | Fran | | | Craig | | |
|---|---|---|---|---|---|---|
| | *Difficulty* | *Time* | *Total* | *Difficulty* | *Time* | *Total* |
| Cooking | 1 | 2 | **3** | 3 | 3 | **6** |
| Food shop | 1 | 1 | **2** | 3 | 2 | **5** |
| Bins | 3 | 2 | **5** | 1 | 1 | **2** |

On the whole, I found cooking the evening meal a joy, a bit
time-consuming but not difficult, whereas Craig found cooking
dinner a horribly stressful chore. However, I hated doing the
bins because I never remembered which bin went out at what
day and it was a mad panic collecting up the bins as the bin
lorry came up the road! Craig found it easy to remember so
the bins caused no stress for him at all.

Our list was extensive! And by the end of the exercise we
were able to divide up the chores. We made sure that not
only were the total scores the same at the end, but that we
had the same number of low-scoring and high-scoring jobs.
We were not doing the same number of jobs at the same
time but by the end of the two weeks we both knew that the
house would be tidy and that we had put in the same amount
of effort as the other.

Some may look at this and think that it is really structured, but we found great freedom within the structure. I didn't feel that I was responsible for everything because I noticed jobs needing doing; Craig didn't get nagged because he didn't. We both had the freedom to do the jobs in our own time and the other person had to trust that they would be done.

This works for us, we happily give and we happily receive; we mostly have a clean, tidy, well-ordered home. I feel loved as I have a husband who does chores without being asked. We have autonomy in our doing with the unwritten rule that the other is not allowed to criticize our work.

*Fran and Craig Walsh*

# 6

## *Marriage and equality*

———•◦•———

Samantha[1] is a gifted leader in her early twenties, an outstanding communicator and a passionate evangelist who loves seeing people come to know Jesus. Working for a Christian organization, she is often the only woman at the meetings she attends and so although she tries hard to empower both men and women, she has a heightened sense of needing to develop women and of creating a doorway for them to join her. She uses the language of 'family' and 'brothers and sisters' a lot, making a point of publicly honouring everyone and deliberately creating a culture of equality where both women and men are valued as unique individuals. Her former boyfriend, however, had very different views, she discovered, about their relationship. In arguments he would end up shouting at her, telling her to submit, claiming that as he was a man he was the head of the household; she didn't need to be included in decisions. She is no longer with him.

There are different understandings among Christians about the roles of women and men in marriage, and while this man's perspective is not unusual I do find it baffling. The creation story clearly shows that women and men were made for relationships of mutuality and partnership, of equality and co-operation. Hierarchy and competition between men and women happened because of the fall and were not what God originally intended. Roy McCloughry says:

> I cannot see how we can talk about a man's authority over a woman being 'natural' since there is nothing natural about a distorted relationship which came about through disobedience.

If we persist in sanctifying the pervasiveness of male power in our world we turn the outcome of the fall into the norm enshrining that which is evil with sacred power.[2]

As followers of Jesus, we are to live out restored relationships, not perpetuate sinful patterns of behaving.

The apostle Paul taught that authority within marriage is mutual and reciprocal; husbands and wives have authority over each other's bodies.[3] He says that the husband is the head of the wife, and although some people interpret this as having to do with authority, many now recognize that the Greek word *kephale* that is translated 'head' was rarely used to mean 'leader' or 'boss' in New Testament times. It's more accurate to understand it as meaning 'source'. Rather than setting up a hierarchy, Paul is affirming that men and women are made of the same stuff, which would have been radical at the time. In Ephesians 5, Paul invites both husbands and wives to love each other sacrificially[4] and to submit to one another out of reverence to Christ.[5] He later emphasizes the need for husbands to love their wives,[6] and for wives to submit to their husbands,[7] but that doesn't cancel out the mutuality of those invitations.

Marriage is a relationship between two adults made in the image of God who commit to living together and loving each other with God's help. Each brings individual gifts, needs, strengths and weaknesses, and together the wife and husband work out how to combine those in a way that enables them to do life faithfully and well, and their particular partnership or family to thrive. Women are not significantly different from men in ways that mean they are somehow deficient or need to be looked after or protected, like they were when they were children. In Genesis 2 and Ephesians 5, a husband and wife are described as being one flesh; the two become one. Marriage is an interdependent relationship of equals, not a hierarchy; each partner wants the other to thrive and to grow towards maturity, not to keep them dependent or immature. At various times each partner will make sacrifices or compromises in order to put the best interests of their partner and their marriage relationship first, but that is not something that is permanently expected of one partner and not the other. Of course there are lots of different ways to relate to each other in marriage, and no blueprint for a successful and happy marriage. The arrangement where a husband is seen as somehow being responsible for decision-making or 'in charge' of the family can work, of course, if both partners willingly choose to follow it, but it is neither necessary nor biblical.

Partners who are married or living together will need to work out what equality looks like in practice for them, and that may not be the same as anyone else. Jonny and I chose to divide all the domestic work between us and were able to job-share when our boys were small; we had almost the same opportunities to work and to look after them. That situation is probably quite rare, although I think there is more scope than people expect for creatively sharing work and the rest of life, and I would encourage people to explore all options. The important thing is to have a foundational commitment to the equality and flourishing of both partners and to keep talking about it. Paul's invitation to us to love each other sacrificially will mean that the focus within the relationship is not on yourself and how well your needs are being met, but on your partner and whether he or she is truly thriving. It means wanting the best for your partner, to see your relationship enabling them to develop and grow and to become more than they could have been if they had remained single. The list of questions on pages 89–90 might help you to explore how both of you feel about the relationship.

Here are some other things to consider as you pursue equality.

## *Start as you mean to go on*

At traditional weddings, women are required to be beautiful, passive and largely silent. Brides are 'given away' by their fathers, a practice that comes from the time when women were regarded as their father's property before marriage and their husband's afterwards. At the reception, the bride listens to speeches by her new husband, his best friend and her dad, where usually thanks are given on her behalf and stories are told about her, but she has no voice. The groom's friends act as ushers who welcome guests and direct them to their seats, while the bride's friends help her with her dress and flowers and provide a colour co-ordinated backdrop to the photos. The groom toasts the bridesmaids for looking gorgeous, and the best man replies on their behalf. The bride throws her bouquet to the female guests, the tradition being that the one who catches it will get married next. While many enjoy these traditions and view them as harmless, an increasing number of people today are choosing to do things differently to reflect the fact that marriage is a celebration of two equal partners coming together. Of course, planning a wedding can be stressful, as you try to negotiate everyone's expectations and desires, so making significant changes to the norm could require tact and diplomacy.

My dad walked me up the aisle, as he had done my sister the year before, a role I didn't want to deprive him of. During the service the minister asked, 'Who brings this woman to be married to this man?' and my dad replied, 'Her mother and I do.' In response to 'Who brings this man to be married to this woman?' the best man, Jonny's brother Dave, said, 'I do.' At the reception we had speeches from my dad, Dave, Jonny, Letty (our best woman), and me – it was important for me to say something on such a significant day, and for my best mate to contribute as well as Jonny's.

It's interesting talking to friends about their weddings, finding out what other people have done. Luke and Caroline were both walked into the ceremony and given away by their fathers. They got married in the round, with their friends all about them. Mark and Anne stood and welcomed guests at the door of the church, and gave each person a flower to pin on their outfits. They then walked up the aisle together to symbolize both walking towards something new. Lis was walked up the aisle by both her parents, and then representatives of her and Dwayne's families did a short 'giving away' speech to reflect the fact that they were each leaving their families and 'cleaving' to each other. What you do needs to suit your personality, of course; there's no point in adding extra stress to the wedding day. Clare felt under pressure to make a speech because it seemed the 'right on' feminist thing to do, but as she hates public speaking she didn't put herself through that ordeal. She and her husband Jon instead chose a female friend to preach at the ceremony, and had traditional speeches. They remember it as a day when they were both able to be their best and play to their strengths.

Traditionally women have taken their husband's surname when they get married, which is what I and my sisters did. It means that my maiden name will die out in our generation; there will be no more Slarks from our part of the family. Taking the man's name can be difficult for many women, who feel that they are giving up an important marker of their identity. There are other options: people may choose to each keep their own surnames, or amalgamate the two; others find creative solutions, like Lis and Dwayne on pages 90–2.

## *Making decisions and mutual submission*

People who are not used to egalitarian marriages will often ask what happens when husband and wife need to make a difficult decision but they have different opinions. If no one has the final say, then how do they move forward?

It's an interesting perspective that you need a hierarchy to make good decisions; I'm not convinced that it's right or healthy. Imagine a couple discussing which school their child should go to. The father favours private education; the mother favours the local comprehensive. They each explain their preference and why they think it's the best for their child. They listen to each other, and talk through the different options. They pray and ask for God's wisdom, sleep on it, come back to the conversation, try to understand where the other is coming from. If you know that ultimately one of you can play the decision-making trump card, then the conversation is unbalanced from the start. Why would you do the hard work of communication, of really listening, questioning and talking, if that can be overruled in an instant? The temptation will be for the conversation to remain superficial because the likely conclusion is already known. Sometimes it's only in the depth of the discussion that you find out exactly why you think the way you do, or you realize how strongly you feel, or you're faced with the flaws in your argument. And isn't it unfair to burden one person in the partnership with the constant need to be right about everything? Far better to both take responsibility and to keep talking until you can reach agreement.

Writing online on this issue, Rosemary Zimmerman, a Quaker, says:

> In Quaker business practice, difficult business and pastoral decisions are made by seeking the will of God and coming to unity on how the Spirit is guiding us. There is no voting. There is no one with a final call. If 30 people in a room can come to unity on a difficult decision like whether to sell a million-dollar property, and 300 people in a room can come to unity on a complicated political position statement (both of which I have seen happen), why should two people in a marriage require hierarchy or a 'shot-caller' to come to unity on anything?[8]

In *The Marriage Book*,[9] Nicky and Sila Lee suggest that it's important for a couple to understand how they differ across personality types, and to appreciate the particular challenges and strengths those differences might bring to the relationship. In terms of decision-making, people can tend towards being an initiator or a supporter, something that is not split along gender lines. They say:

> Initiators enjoy coming up with new ideas, make decisions easily, and are not afraid of change. They like to take charge, and make good leaders. Supporters like others to take the initiative. They listen carefully and hesitate to express their opinions. They prefer to avoid confrontation and are prepared to adapt their own preferences to maintain harmony. In order to obtain the right balance of leadership and support, there are two dangers to avoid. Initiators can fail to consult their partner. Supporters may defer all responsibility for decisions to their husband or wife. Neither tendency is healthy in a marriage, as each partner should be included in all decisions

which affect them as a couple. It is worth remembering that 'leadership' does not mean dominating, controlling or imposing our own agenda. Nor does 'supporting' mean following passively or remaining unheard . . . Marriages work best when each partner initiates in some areas, and supports their husband or wife in others.

In practice, people discover ways of reaching decisions depending on the issue being discussed. It might be appropriate to let the person with the most knowledge make the decision; sometimes it needs to be the person who will be most affected; at other times the one who is less bothered might give way to the one who cares deeply. Someone might choose to let go of a preference and submit to the other person, knowing that at another time it could go the other way. If there's a complete impasse, then perhaps it's a sign of something unhealthy in the relationship that needs to be addressed. Letting one partner automatically make the decision in that situation won't allow that work to happen. Talking things through together with a trusted friend who can give an outside perspective can be helpful.

You need to take into consideration the significance of the decision. When it's just about personal preference and isn't really that important, Jonny and I have sometimes tossed a coin to decide. For example, when we decorated our kitchen I thought the skirting board should be cream and he thought it should be white. We decided to toss a coin and whoever won could choose the colour but would also do the painting. We had a beautifully painted white skirting board. At other times, the decision has bigger implications. When I was pregnant with our second child, we couldn't decide on a name if the baby was a boy. Jonny preferred Harry; I favoured Toby. We talked and talked but weren't getting anywhere so I decided to 'try out' the name Harry for a couple of weeks. I imagined a little boy called Harry, practised talking to him, tested the name out alongside our older son's, Joel, and I found that it wasn't so bad after all. I let go of wanting to call the baby Toby, and now I think Harry has a great name that fits him perfectly. The most serious disagreement we had was whether we could manage without a lodger to help pay the mortgage. I felt our boys needed more space as they got older and we could afford to live without the rent coming in. Jonny disagreed and was concerned about turfing our friend out of his room. We had some difficult conversations where I felt he wasn't really listening; at one point I flounced out of a pub, leaving him on his own, when we tried to talk about it: not my finest hour. But we kept talking, listening, praying until we reached an agreement to try it for a year to see if we could afford it.

An attitude of mutual submission doesn't mean that you both sit there like doormats saying 'I don't mind'. It does mean that you approach conversations with humility; you explain your perspective assertively but not aggressively; you listen intently and ask questions to make sure you've understood correctly; you weigh up carefully the possibility that you could be wrong; you consider how you might compromise and you actively seek the flourishing of your partner, wanting to see them learn, grow and develop to their full potential. And it means that you pray, a lot.

## Work and careers

The model of the man as breadwinner and the woman as homemaker has only been practised in limited sectors of western society for limited periods of time. Throughout history other patterns have existed of men and women working alongside each other in both paid and unpaid work to provide in different ways for their families. Work is a good part of God's creation, a way of using our gifts and skills to develop creation and contribute to the greater good. At its best, work can be a source of fulfilment and an opportunity to make the world a better place. Add to that the fact that in the UK, the reality for most couples is that they both need to work to make ends meet and you can see that the breadwinner/homemaker model is unrealistic for most; it is just one choice out of many rather than an ideal to aim for.

In the Sermon on the Mount, Jesus tells us not to be obsessed with what we will eat, drink or wear and invites us to make the kingdom of God our priority, to trust God for what we need rather than in our own ability to provide for ourselves. We have an opportunity to see work as a way of using the gifts God has given us to serve rather than a means of gaining status, significance or wealth. Jesus challenges our definition of a successful career – is it one where you've progressed as far as you can and achieved and earned as much as you can, or one where you've worked hard to follow your calling? Conversations about who does what in terms of work should centre not around who can earn the most, although clearly there's a need for your partnership or family to be sustainable, but how each of you is being obedient to God's call and whether you are thriving and growing.

Most couples experience an ebb and flow over the years of whose work or passion takes priority and whose will be laid down for a season if necessary. Rather than assuming that one person's career will always take precedence, couples need to keep an open mind, sometimes stepping back from their own work to support the other, and sometimes being the one who follows an opportunity. Here are some examples of how other people have handled this.

- Lowell and Kande are from Canada originally, but came to England shortly after they got married because Lowell felt called to work here. Twenty years later, Lowell left his job as leader of Youth for Christ to follow Kande to Japan, as she felt that God was strongly calling her to minister there. Kande was born in Japan to missionary parents so it was a second home to her, whereas Lowell didn't know the language and initially didn't have a specific role there.[10]
- Nick and Bridget ran a youth organization together, but when Bridget was accepted for ordination in the Anglican Church, Nick took on the role of being the main carer for their children while Bridget studied at theological college. Nick says that it was obvious to him that he could take a break from work and still be connected, career-wise, much more easily than Bridget could. He did a PhD while his children were small and is now leader of a youth work training organization.
- Iain and Sonia both worked a three-day week while their children were small so that they could share work and hands-on parenting.

Iain is a self-employed sculptor, which gave him a lot of flexibility, while Sonia works for a children's charity. Over the past eight years Sonia has studied for a degree and an MA alongside working, so there have been times when Iain has needed to pick up more of the work of running the home. At other times, Sonia has carried a greater part of the load at home to give Iain opportunities to develop his artwork and his career.

## *And the rest . . .*

There are many other issues where a commitment to equality will affect the way you approach the subject and the decisions you make about it. Be intentional about practising equality in each of these areas, rather than reverting to default settings that you haven't deliberately chosen. *The Marriage Book* by Nicky and Sila Lee has excellent advice on how to work at a committed relationship.

### Money

Money is one of the subjects most likely to cause conflict or stress in a relationship. If you are the main earner, how can you avoid the feeling that the money is 'yours' rather than 'ours'? How can you celebrate and value the unpaid contributions that individuals make to the well-being of the family, such as looking after the home or caring for children? How can you share responsibility for budgeting, spending, saving, reconciling and debt, even if one partner is more skilled at dealing with the finances? At a practical level, it's important that you both know passwords for bank accounts and other details in case anything happens to your partner.

### Social glue

Asda's advert for Christmas 2012 showed a valiant mum working her fingers to the bone to make Christmas perfect for her family, while the rest of them looked on. It attracted a lot of criticism for portraying dads as passive and lazy and mums as self-righteous martyrs, but it did at least highlight the work that goes into the social glue that keeps families and friends together. How can you share responsibility for those actions that build relationships within a family and community – remembering birthdays and anniversaries, for example, buying cards and presents, inviting people round for meals and cooking, and making arrangements to celebrate events like Christmas?

## Sex

There are lots of myths around about men, women and sex – that men think about sex every seven seconds, that women need more of an emotional connection to enjoy sex, that men are aroused more quickly, that women have a lower sex drive. While some myths may contain an element of truth, it's important to learn about your own partner's preferences and responses rather than expecting generalizations to be true. As I've said before, there is huge diversity among men and among women and that diversity will show much more strongly in a relationship of just two people. Good communication is key, as is a commitment to learning about and learning to please your partner.

### Talking about flourishing

Questions like the ones listed below can form one way of exploring how each of you feels about the relationship you are in and whether you are both thriving within it. It's unlikely that you'll both be able to answer all the questions positively, particularly if you have small children or other demands on your time, but there needs to be some balance between you in the number of areas where life feels good. Talk about which areas are most important to you and which need addressing. What could you do to help each other to thrive?

- What meaningful work do you have to do where you feel you are using your gifts and skills (which might not be paid employment)?
- When do you have time to yourself that you can choose how you spend?

- What is your creative outlet, an opportunity to make something?
- How do you feel you are contributing to the well-being of this relationship or family?
- Who are the good friends you are able to spend time with, who enrich your life?
- If you have children, when are you totally responsible for your children's well-being? When are you able to rest from that responsibility?
- What opportunities do you have to exercise and to pursue health?
- When do you get to do the things you love doing, that make your heart sing?
- When do you feel taken for granted?
- In what ways are you connected to the local community?
- How do you feel that you are learning and growing?
- What dreams for the future are you currently pursuing?

### It's all in the name

About six months after we started going out with each other we were at a football match with some friends when one of them started to quiz us on where our relationship was going and what surname we would use when we got married. In the conversation that followed, we realized that neither of us assumed that we would take on Dwayne's surname, even though that was what most of our friends were doing and it was certainly the norm in our parents' generation. We started to explore other options.

We knew that in Sweden the couple usually chooses between the surnames and that it's about 50:50 as to whose they pick. We knew couples who had hyphenated their two names into one, and also of one or two who had merged their two names to form a new word or come up with a new name altogether. So, we certainly didn't invent what we ended up doing.

Our original surnames were Hickman and Ford. We tried to amalgamate them in some way but couldn't find a combination that worked. We then took a different approach and tried to find words in other languages that meant something that we were passionate about. One name that came up was Baraka, a word we'd first come across because it is the name of a movie. The film is a sequence of images from many cultures with a fabulous soundtrack, but no dialogue or typical storyline. We thought that the movie is a profound showcase of humanity and all its strengths and frailties. The word Baraka means 'blessing', usually in the sense of a blessing from God, in languages such as Arabic and Swahili. At special celebrations people wish others 'baraka', often accompanied by big gestures, hugs and almost always exclamation marks! Baraka is a contemporary French term for luck. Berakhah is Hebrew for blessing. Barraca is the Spanish word for a hut, home or farmhouse. Baraka means hut in Croatian or Bulgarian. After further thinking and waiting to see how we felt about it, we agreed that it was the one we wanted. We did 'test out' the word with a few people from Arabic and Swahili communities before taking it on. They always responded really warmly to the meaning it conjured up for them, so that encouraged us to go ahead with it.

We didn't announce our new name at our wedding because we wanted to be absolutely sure about it before going ahead. When we were ready, we sent out invitations to a party where we would sign our 'change of name' documents (in Australia, that's the legal process of arranging the change; nothing happens automatically on marriage).

In response to our announcement, we got some hugely positive comments. Those who didn't like the idea mainly kept their views to themselves, although a few seemed bemused by our decision. Members of our family responded in various ways – from indifference to puzzlement to something close to anger. Some thought that we were rejecting our past, or that we must be trying to escape from something, or to create some new and better life by giving ourselves a new name.

We tried to point out that we weren't expecting a change of name to change anything about the past or the future; we knew that a change of name couldn't heal anything even if we wanted it to. We also assumed that it wouldn't harm anything either, although perhaps others should be the judge of that. For us, it was a symbol of a new life and family together but there was nothing particularly magical or mystical about it. It all felt very simple and normal. In our experience, people who know what the word means have been curious about how we have the name and then amazed and delighted about our story.

*Lis and Dwayne Baraka*

# 7

## *Parenting and equality*

———— ·•·•·•· ————

Parenting is a huge responsibility. If we really understood the enormity of what we were embarking on, the nurturing of a human life from completely dependent newborn to almost independent young adult ready to take on the world, I wonder how many of us would do it. Parenting is an amazing privilege that's hugely rewarding and enjoyable, but it's also hard work and requires selflessness, sacrifice and maturity. No wonder God made the creation of a new life dependent on the love and co-operation of two people; this is something we need to do together.

Families come in all shapes and sizes. In our community we have just celebrated the creation of two new families – a couple who have been approved for adoption who will hopefully soon be mum and dad to a pair of siblings, and a grandma who has been made kinship carer for her grandson after he'd spent most of his life in foster care. My friends who are single parents find conversations about equality largely academic because they just get on with doing what's needed, whether that's traditionally the mum's role or the dad's or falls somewhere in between. None of us brings up our children in isolation from our wider communities; aunts, uncles, grandparents, youth workers, godparents and good friends all help to nurture our children and teach them what it is to be girls and boys, women and men. So although for shorthand through this chapter I talk mainly about mums and dads, I hope you'll be able to apply it to your family relationships, whatever their structure and whatever role you play.

I may be sounding like a stuck record by now, but there is no one model for how to practise equality in parenting. It's much more about attitude and intention, and what works for the particular context of your family. Some couples are able to split everything almost evenly between them, and that's certainly worth exploring, but that's not the only way to do it. A decision to share parenting equally is the agreement that the responsibility rests equally with both of you, that neither will have overall control or expertise, that you want to resist default patterns, that you want to model something liberating for your children in terms of what it says about men and women, and that you'll practise equality and respect. What's important is to sit down and talk about how you share parenting, and review regularly to see if you're enacting what you decided. The tips for conversations on pages 74–6 and the questions about sharing life on pages 89–90 might be useful. But there are definitely some common themes to consider. We've looked at sharing housework, which is very important; let's explore three other areas in a similar way: child-raising, work, and time for self.[1]

## *Child-raising*

At one level, you become a parent when you have a baby with someone, but it takes more than that to be an involved, engaged parent who is actively sharing in the adventure of raising a child. I have a friend who, when I invite her out for an evening, invariably says that she'll see if her husband can babysit. With a smile, I remind her that looking after your own children is called parenting. The 'dads as babysitters' approach to parenting – allowing them to fill in only when the mum isn't around – can put them in the margins of their own children's lives. At its most extreme, it means that some married women, out of choice or necessity, are effectively single parents because they do most of the work of raising their children.

Child-raising is about the practical caring for children's needs, making sure they eat healthily, sleep and exercise enough, have clean clothes, have friends round to play, and so on. It's also about enabling them to develop emotionally, socially, spiritually, morally, physically and intellectually. In order to do any of that well, I believe that it helps to be involved in all of it. First, so much of our children's development takes place as life happens, not in planned moments. Rather than scheduling in a long conversation about sex when they are aged ten, it's far more effective to answer questions, use opportunities around you and pick up on comments as they happen from early childhood, so they are learning little and often and can integrate new information with what they already know. And second, it's in the hands-on stuff, in the doing of things together, the sharing of joys and frustrations, that relationships are built, developed, tested and thrive. Children learn from doing things with you and seeing how you cope with the everyday much more than they do from what you say to them; having two hands-on involved parents can only enrich their lives. Here are some things to consider as you talk about how to share child-raising.

## Both of you need to learn how to do it

You don't become an expert parent as soon as you give birth to your baby; it's something you have to learn, whether you are a woman or a man. Pregnancy perhaps gives women a head start because they can't escape the fact that a new life is on its way, and usually they are thrown in at the deep end once they've given birth. They may have time in hospital to be on their own with the baby; they are trying to establish feeding and coping with an utterly dependent baby. Although it takes women different lengths of time to bond with their babies, after just a few days they can seem to be the experts in changing a nappy and settling a crying infant in a moment; dads can be left trying to catch up. New mums need to give new dads space to learn for themselves how to look after the baby, and resist telling them what to do or taking over. Obviously only mums can breastfeed, so particularly in the early weeks and months they will end up doing more of the practical care. Many women take maternity leave, which again gives them opportunity to become the expert parent, but you don't have to let those two things set the pattern for the next 18 years. On pages 106–7, Lisa Raine Hunt talks about how she and her husband reset the balance of practical caring for their son so that they could both be fully involved. Do you need to do something similar?

## Aim to do everything sometimes

It makes sense to share out responsibilities and opportunities according to your interests, time available and skills. In one sense, it doesn't matter if that conforms to traditional roles. Jonny was always much better at playing football in the park with our boys; I didn't really care enough about it whereas he loved it. If we want to subvert some of the gender stereotypes constantly seen around us, however, and open up opportunities for our children, then we need to mix things up a bit and demonstrate the range of what we can do rather than leaving particular activities down to just one parent. If one of you does most of the cooking, make sure the other makes a meal for the family on a regular basis. If one of you clears out the garage, the other could take the accumulated rubbish to the tip. I confess I never got over my apathy towards football, but I did my bit as an active mum: I introduced my boys to triathlons, organizing a mini one in the pool and park for their friends.

## Share the bad times and the good

From time to time, children get ill, wake up with nightmares, wet the bed, throw up everywhere, fall out with friends and get into trouble at school. Aim to share in dealing with these challenges as well as in all the joys. Take it in turns to stay at home from work when one of your children is ill, even if one employer is less sympathetic to that than the other. Alternate who gets up in the night to care for the children, particularly if you're both going to work the next day. For months when Joel was a baby he would wake several times in the night; then, when he did sleep through he would wake up regularly at 5 a.m. We had a strict rota for who would get up with him! If your child has a series of GP or hospital appointments, it may make sense for just one of you to do it for continuity's sake, but consider how you can keep your partner involved and informed.

## Hands-on parents who work full time

It's harder for both of you to be committed to sharing parenting equally if one of you is working and the other stays at home with the children. It's easy for the working parent to feel disconnected and for the at-home parent to end up doing everything. You need to be intentional about the working parent plunging back into hands-on parenting at the end of the day and during weekends. When we job-shared, on my working days I would play with the boys when I came home while Jonny cooked dinner, and then I would do bath and bedtime while he washed up – and vice versa. Martin Saunders talks on pages 104–5 about how he stays hands-on as a parent as well as working full time.

## *Work*

For decades women have been caught up in the 'mummy wars', with arguments going back and forth about whether they should stay at home with their children or go back to work and pursue their careers. Whatever they decide, women can feel guilty – for not contributing financially or not using their education if they stay at home, or for leaving their children with child-minders if they go out to work. Christians can intensify the animosity by adding a theological veneer about 'what God wants for us', which is usually for women to be at home. In fact, a variety of models of family life are described in the Bible, and few of them look like the breadwinning father/stay-at-home mother model promoted in some sections of the Church. The Proverbs 31 woman is often held up as the ideal but she can be seen as an unattainable paragon that makes women everywhere feel guilty for underperforming. I think it's more accurate to see the Proverbs 31 woman as a composite picture of all that women can achieve between them, in which case the Bible honours women for the different roles they contribute, as strong, wise, successful businesswomen, leaders, parents, carers, craftswomen, merchants, providers and teachers, able to cope with whatever life throws at them.[2] There is space in the kingdom of God for mothers who stay at home with their children *and* for mothers who go out to work, and I wish the Church would affirm that more. There is no right or wrong way; people make decisions about going back to work for all sorts of reasons and some have little choice; life is expensive.

Work is about more than earning money; in the last chapter I said that work is a good part of God's creation, a way of using our gifts and skills to develop creation and contribute to the greater good. At its best, work can be a source of fulfilment and an opportunity to make the world a better place. Both parents need to be 'working' in the sense of using their gifts and feeling that they are making a valuable contribution to the family and the wider community, and for some that will mean staying at home to look after children full time. It's really important to value what an at-home parent contributes to family life, irrespective of whether they make a financial contribution. It can be helpful in that sense to see raising children as someone's 'work', as the primary place where that parent is called to be for this season of life. We also need to be aware of the power dynamics that often accompany money, and how easy it is to value earning above other contributions; the tendency to think that money makes up for lack of parental involvement should be resisted. Consider the following as you talk about how both of you will weave together employment, earning, caring for children and pursuing your callings.

## Take the opportunity to rethink things

Having a child transforms your life; you will never be the same again. With so much changing, this is an opportunity to rethink priorities and explore possibilities. For the first few years, your children need as much of your time as you are able to give them; once they are at school, though, you'll have a bit more freedom. How could you approach this next season of life so that all of you can thrive? Not everyone can share work and parenting, but I am convinced that there are more creative opportunities to be explored if we take the time and don't make assumptions about who will do what.

Take as much parental leave as you are entitled to while your children are small. Dads are given only two weeks of statutory paternity leave but some employers are more generous. Parental leave can now be shared; dads can take up to 26 weeks of parental leave if the mother of their child has returned to work.[3] Financially, consider how much you really need to earn over the next few years. Some people don't have any choice, but could you reduce your hours at work for a season in order to spend more time with your children? Employers' attitudes vary as to how supportive they are of working parents, but ask around and find out what colleagues have done. All employees who care for someone have a right to request flexible working, not just mums who are returning to work.[4] If you can't afford to reduce the number of hours you work, can you work compressed hours, in order to have one day a week at home? Can you work from home from time to time, to free up the hours you would spend commuting. Keep an eye on the future for both of you; will it be easier for one of you than the other to step back into full-time working when your children are older? If so, it might be wise for that partner to work less now. Is there some way you could keep connected to your area of work while you spend time at home, through study or peer groups or courses, so you don't lose out on knowledge or experience? Your gifts and calling don't disappear when you become a parent, and however much time you spend with your children, you'll be a better parent for having an outlet to use your skills and be involved in what you're passionate about.

If you both divide your time between work and childcare, it helps to have established routines so that everyone knows where they stand. Bridget says:

> We have designated days on which we each do the school run. On those days the person who picks up the children is responsible for after-school activities and making a family meal. We also regularly make use of teenage babysitters from church if our work or social diaries clash and we're both out at the same time. That way there isn't an expectation that one person should defer to the other.

Jonny and I found it important to have regular 'diary meetings' where we talked about who was doing what over the next few months, and to get into the habit of never committing to anything until we'd checked what the other was doing.

## Choosing childcare

Choosing a good environment for your child to be in while you're at work is a very personal thing. Some families are able to call on grandparents, or share childcare with friends; others use child-minders, au pairs, nannies or nurseries. The ideal is to have consistency, with lots of adult interaction, with people you trust who have similar values to you. The key thing is to make even this a shared activity. Often when men have children their work lives continue as if nothing has happened; their children are invisible at work. When women return to work after having children, they are still likely to carry the responsibility for childcare. It's seen as something that enables the mother to work, rather than enabling both parents to work. The costs are compared to the mother's salary to see if it is worth doing, rather than deducted from both parents' salaries. The woman does all the organizing and problem-solving, such as when the child-minder is ill, rather than both parents being involved. Men have an opportunity to change the culture of their workplaces by showing a holistic approach to work and parenting, and being open with their colleagues that they are dads with responsibilities for children.

## Dads as stay-at-home parents

An increasing number of dads are taking time out of their careers to look after their children – although they are still in the minority. A 2011 survey suggested that 6 per cent of British fathers are stay-at-home dads, which represents a tenfold increase over the past ten years.[5] It's worth serious consideration, although it's not an easy option. Neil has been the primary carer for his children since they were born, while his wife Amanda has been employed as a youth worker and now as a teacher. He's found it an amazing experience to spend so much time with his children, but also a challenge at times to be a man in a predominantly female world. He says, 'The praise that I have sometimes received from women for doing the job that women have been expected to do for generations has been interesting.' Other people have made it clear that in their opinion he should get back to work because he is a man.

Men going down this route will need to be secure in who they are, and able to find solutions to problems of isolation and at times boredom. But then, that's no different from what women may experience when they stop work to look after children.

## You don't know until you do it

I read lots of parenting and baby books before I had children and had an idea of what I thought parenting would be like, but nothing really prepares you for the reality. I was surprised at the depth of love I had for my son Joel, but I didn't find being at home with a newborn baby easy. It was a very lonely experience, and I lost all confidence in my abilities to do anything much. I'd always intended to go back to work after six to nine months, but I began to doubt whether I could. After talking it through with Jonny, he gave me the push I needed; after three months of maternity leave, I went back to work for two days a week while Jonny stayed at home on those days to look after Joel. That was what worked for us; others will find different solutions. While it's important to plan, you also need to retain some flexibility to see how the experience of being a parent changes you.

## *Time to self*

Having time to yourself may seem like an impossible dream when you have a baby, but it's an important beacon of hope to hold on to. All parents need some time when they have sole responsibility for their children, and all parents need some time when they have no responsibility for their children. Stay-at-home parents can find themselves craving adult conversation, or even just the opportunity to visit the bathroom by themselves without a small child attached. Going to work, while challenging in a different way, can feel like a welcome break from the incessant demands of a toddler.

So make sure you both have time to yourselves, where you can pursue your own interests and just do what you like. A working parent might do a regular activity with the kids at the weekend to give the home parent time for self; they could meet up again later to do family stuff. It can be hard to balance everything, and often time to yourself drops to the bottom of a parent's priorities, but I always found that it made me a better parent so you owe it to your family to protect it fiercely. Time to yourself is where you recharge your batteries, remember who you are and dream for the future.

There's one more issue linked to parenting that's important to consider if we want to create a world where our children can be free to be themselves. And it's not only parents who need to take note – aunts, uncles, grandparents and adult friends all have an opportunity to contribute either positively or negatively.

## *Helping children negotiate stereotypes*

There was a brilliant advert in the 1970s that showed a little girl, in blue jeans and stripy T-shirt, proudly holding a complex building made out of Lego with the slogan 'what it is is beautiful'. The copy talked about the need for children to be creative and the pride they take in making things. Now Lego marketing targets girls with pink buckets of bricks and *Friends* building sets that feature girls in stereotypical settings. When you walk into shops catering for children, whether it's clothes, toys, books or games, it can feel as if boys and girls are brought up in separate worlds, with girls cocooned in pink and boys expected to be active, independent and strong. A set of magnetic words for the fridge door is available, designed to help children with literacy.[6] A pink set for girls includes the words make-up, hairband, party, princess, diamond and angel, while the blue set for boys has glue, monster, scary, mud, frogs and football. The only words in common are sweets and bubbles. Is that really the only overlap between boys and girls? These types of toys help to construct gender and close down our children's options.

The excellent campaign Let Toys be Toys[7] highlights the way that marketing to children limits their interests and their choices. Children are very sensitive to what's expected of their own sex, and what they are 'allowed' to do as boys and as girls. Writing on their blog, Tricia Lowther talks about how her daughter loves the

Disney film *Cars*. Tricia bought some cartons of drinks decorated with the characters and put one in her daughter's lunchbox for school, only for her daughter to take it out again saying she was embarrassed. Tricia says, 'After a bit of coaxing she told me it was because *Cars* is "boyish". When I said to her that I thought she liked *Cars*, she said, very quietly, "I do, but I don't want anyone to know."'[8] The campaign targets retailers who separate toys into unnecessary and restrictive gendered categories, and encourages them to stop being so exclusive. Hamleys toy shop in London used to segregate toys for boys and toys for girls by floor, but in 2011, following pressure from parents, began organizing toys by type rather than by who they thought should play with them. Other retailers are now doing the same.

Adults can respect children's preferences while also helping them to deconstruct adverts and stereotypes, and deliberately expanding their horizons. Sonia has two daughters:

> From when they were a young age we were really conscious about not following the usual stereotypes, such as only giving them traditional girls' toys. They both had cars, dolls, trains and a whole range of things to play with. Our eldest daughter did really like dolls and our youngest loved pirates! But they both knew boys and girls could play with the same things. We also intentionally challenged stereotypes through the stories we read them, for example *Princess Smarty Pants* and *Prince Cinder* by Babette Cole and *Paperbag Princess* by Robert Munsch.

Another mother, Rachel, has recently discovered that her toddler is obsessed with princesses, so she makes a point of teaching her that princesses are brave, bright and kind.

It also matters how we talk to children. Mark notices that at his church adults will tend to comment on his young daughter's appearance more than anything else, while they never do that to his sons.

> They'll say things like, 'You look very pretty today,' or 'That's a lovely dress.' I know they're only trying to make conversation but if that's the only thing we commend girls for, or

always the first thing that we notice, aren't we giving girls a rather damaging message that mirrors what they pick up from the rest of our culture – that what matters is the way these little girls look, that if they want approval or attention then they need to look pretty?

There are other ways to make a connection, which might include, 'What are you reading at the moment?', 'Have you been doing anything fun today?', 'What was your favourite thing at school this week?' and so on.

## Raising the next generation

If we want to see change, then it really matters how we bring up the next generation in terms of what we model, how we help children to understand the world they are living in, and what opportunities we open up for them. The proof of our ability to share life equally as women and men will be seen in large part in what our children and grandchildren consider to be normal: what their default settings are at work, in the home and in relationships. I'm watching with interest.

### Full-time employee and full-time dad

My alarm goes off at 5.45 each morning. If I'd known, aged 18, that this was what being a grown-up entailed, I'd have been much less keen on becoming one. I do this because I work in central London (where I don't live), and this is the only way to ensure that I can spend a decent amount of time with my children every day. I get home in time to help them eat dinner, to bath them and to read them stories. I do this because I love them, because I know that the strongest upbringing they can receive is from two committed parents, and because while my nearly-12-hour working day involves sleepy train journeys and uninterrupted trips to the local coffee shop, my wife's nearly-12-hour working day is non-stop.

Raising children is a full-time occupation. You might choose to subcontract that work to a nursery, nanny or enthusiastic grandparent, but to do it well is to do it all the time. Children's emotional, physical and developmental needs don't let up for a second. I am in awe of the input that my wife – a trained and accomplished primary school teacher – invests in our children, but I don't for one moment consider my full-time occupation to be the 'real' job that enables her to play mum. We both work full time. We both contribute to raising our children *and* to my ability to travel to an office each day. When money got tighter at one point, my wife returned to work for two days a week, and I was part of the childcare 'solution' that we came up with (a six-month period that left me in no doubt about who had the easier job).

The area in which we live is extremely affluent (we're called to be misfits there!). The people who live alongside us are generally materially rich, but time poor. On the occasions that I've had to work late, I've travelled home in train carriages full of those same men I see on the 6.20 a.m. service, many of whom I know to be parents. In the lucrative pursuit of a city job, they relinquish the chance of seeing their children during the week. I also know that at least a few of them are keen and regular weekend golfers. In the pursuit of relaxation and of spending their hard-earned rewards, they relinquish the chance of seeing their children at the weekend too.

My children need to see me every day, far more than they need an annual holiday to Disneyland. It's much more important that I'm around regularly than it is that we have everything we want. They also need to understand that their mum and dad are an equal partnership, working and parenting together. Getting up at 5.45 each morning is the best strategy I have for being the best role model to them that I can.

*Martin Saunders, editor of* Youthwork *magazine*[9]

## Learning to let go

Equality for me has always begun at home. Not only between the sexes, but between all people; those from different cultural backgrounds, of different faiths, disabled and able, the list is long . . . If women and men do not experience equality in the most vulnerable and formative location of our day-to-day lives, how can we carry it into our churches, workplaces and communities?

I don't think we can presume what equality might look like in the home. Equality does not necessitate homogeneity; an important part of equality for me is an understanding and nurturing of individuality. While my dad manages the finances in my parents' home and my mum does all the cooking, in our home my husband hates figures so I keep an eye on the accounts, and when my work took up a fair amount of time in the evening my husband did the cooking, although he didn't particularly enjoy it. Roles in the two households might be polar opposites in some respects, but this does not define the equality experienced.

The arrival of our son Oscar set a new challenge as to what equality might look like in our family unit. We both led an incredibly full life with long hours at work and a packed diary. We are both blessed with an amazing network of friends and family, but while I had grown up in a hands-on church community, looking after the children of friends since I was a child myself, my husband could count the number of times he had held a baby on one hand (perhaps even one finger). Jackson was a practical and committed dad from the outset, not lacking in willingness to change nappies, wash, feed and care for Oscar, only the confidence to do so on his own. While I was on maternity leave it was practical for me to take on the majority of care for our son, but we quickly realized that this was not sustainable if I was to return to work. To fit in my freelance work around spending some time at home with Oscar, I would also need to work in the evenings, which meant that Jackson might need to lead in some areas I had taken care of.

A tricky and at times painful couple of months followed for both of us as we relearned our roles in our marriage, giving up tasks we had previously enjoyed and taking on new patterns that at the time didn't seem particularly appealing. The biggest challenge for me was to give up control. I am fastidious and Jackson is not; I love cooking and cleaning; Jackson does not. I needed to learn that meals don't always come in three courses and that a small flat with a small baby may never be spotlessly clean. The only way we changed was by dropping ourselves in at the deep end. Although we have a wonderful child-minder, we arranged some days where Jackson would take holiday and look after Oscar, so he could get to grips with a full day of childcare. We persevered through many a fraught phone call and a fair few arguments and at the other side I think we are much closer as a result. Jackson better understands my exhausting six months' maternity leave and my rush home from work in the evening to collect and feed Oscar, and I understood his challenge of working a full day in the office and then switching into family mode and working a full evening at home in a completely different role with a tired and cranky wife! We are different people now. I am more relaxed than I have ever been, I don't over-commit our diary and I leave space for the three of us to be together at weekends to share our very different weeks. Jackson has discovered that he even enjoys cooking on occasion – so long as he can listen to a football podcast undisturbed while doing so.

*Lisa Raine Hunt*

# 8

## *Work and equality*

————•◆•————

It's an innocent question; it usually comes up when you're getting to know someone new – 'So what do you do for work?' Usually it's a way of getting people to talk about their lives and what's important to them, to find out more about what makes them tick. But it can spark existential questions – is my worth defined by what I do or how much I earn? If I'm not employed or not earning, does that mean I'm not working? Who decided that 'work' and 'employment' should mean the same thing?

Before talking about equality and work, I want to say that there are very few people who don't work. My mum, for example, has worked hard all her life but most of that has not been in paid employment. She was a domestic science teacher when she first got married; she left to have four children in fairly quick succession. For the next 12 years her work was bringing up her daughters, running the home and getting involved in church and community life. When I was 11, we moved into a home for retired missionaries and lived with them in community. For six years my mum's work was to manage the well-being of this extended family and care for all its members' different needs, still unpaid. Later, when my dad took early retirement, she set up her own successful business making soft furnishings and became a member of the Guild of Master Craftsmen, this time earning money again. For three years she was a full-time carer for my dad as he became more frail, working hard to juggle carers, meals and doctors to make sure the end of his life was comfortable and full of love. I don't believe that work is synonymous with paid employment or that anyone should describe themselves as 'just' a stay-at-home parent. But for the purposes of this chapter and for ease of reading, I use the word 'work' to mean paid employment. I hope you will keep this start to the chapter in mind as you read.

## *Practising gender at work*

Most of us will go out to work at some point in our lives, exchanging our skills, creativity and muscle power for money that helps us to live. Some people are employed by organizations, some run their own businesses, some work freelance for different people. Some of us have clear boundaries between work and the rest of our lives, while for others the distinction is more fluid. Wherever you work, it's interesting to think about how that experience of working interacts with who you are – how you change your workplace and how your workplace changes you, particularly, for our purposes, in the area of gender.

As people have studied how workplaces function and how that impacts the people who work within them, there has been a growing realization that organizations are not gender-neutral. We might think that gender is something that people bring in to work from outside but that view ignores the way that workplaces have developed. Joan Acker, who has studied gender and organizations, says that 'law, politics, religion, the academy, the state, and the economy are institutions historically developed by men, currently dominated by men, and symbolically interpreted from the standpoint of men in leading positions'.[1] In previous generations, the traditional workplace depended on an anonymous worker, who was assumed to be a man, doing an abstract job. Work and family life were kept completely separate and didn't encroach on each other. This worker was able to be completely devoted to his full-time job because his wife, or mother or housekeeper took care of his personal needs and his children. Although the world of work has changed significantly, some of those same expectations still linger. Acker argues that far from being neutral, organizations are gendered, meaning that:

> advantage and disadvantage, exploitation and control, action and emotion, meaning and identity, are patterned through and

in terms of a distinction between male and female, masculine and feminine. Gender is not an addition to ongoing processes, conceived as gender neutral. Rather, it is an integral part of those processes, which cannot be properly understood without an analysis of gender.[2]

We have already explored how gender can be constructed through interactions with other people, through the messages and models we absorb from society, and from which of our actions are affirmed by others and which are punished. Patricia Yancey Martin also talks about practising gender: the way we live out our beliefs about men and women in our actions and words, the 'literal sayings and doings of gender in real time and place'. This happens in every area of life, including work. So, for example, men who refer to women in the workplace as 'girls' are practising gender, by infantilizing women in the language they choose. Women who work better for a male manager and resist being managed by another woman are practising gender by favouring the leadership of men. Men who only mentor other men at work are practising gender by acting in the belief that having that type of working relationship with a woman is risky. In all these examples, people are enacting their beliefs about women and men in their words and behaviour at work. Work is not a neutral place that men and women enter and leave without it having any impact on their experience of being men and women. The practising of gender at work helps to shape who we are and how we feel about ourselves as women and men.

## Exploring the experiences of women and men at work

The study of gender and work throws up a complex and contradictory picture. On the one hand it's possible to identify several ways in which women are still disadvantaged in the workplace – lower wages, higher unemployment, greater responsibility for unpaid labour, under-representation in positions of authority and leadership, lower autonomy and control over work, lower expectations of promotion, and the way that the recession has disproportionately affected women.

But in contrast, some women achieve high-profile, powerful positions in a number of sectors. They are able to break through the glass ceiling and overcome the discrimination and barriers that hold other women back. In conversations about gender and organizations, there's a temptation to simplify arguments – for example that men choose other men for senior positions – when the reality is more complex and conflicting, with evidence that women sometimes prefer to have men in managerial positions. Nevertheless, from all that has been written about gender and organizations, there is agreement about the 'extraordinary persistence through history and across societies of the subordination of women'.[3]

The widespread belief that men and women are, and should be, completely different from each other also plays out in the workplace. Studies show that the way a behaviour is interpreted depends on whether it is performed by women or men.[4] Men are expected to be confident and self-promoting, whereas overt displays of competence and confidence by women can get a negative response; more modest women may be commended because that behaviour accords with stereotypical feminine norms. Sheryl Sandberg notes that as a woman becomes more successful she is less liked, and as a man becomes more successful he is more liked.[5]

That belief in essential differences can affect the type of jobs that men and women pursue. Women in the UK are rarely taken on for jobs that require physical strength, despite the fact that tests have shown that a nurse's job can require as much expenditure of energy in a typical shift as mining or fishing.[6] Anyone who has lived in or even just visited a developing country will see very different expectations of the physical strength of women, who often farm the land by hand and carry water for long distances. Elaine Storkey tells the story of a trip to Ethiopia in her role as President of Tearfund. She was met at the airport by a group of men and women. The men welcomed her and shook her hand while the women picked up her cases, put them on their heads and carried them to the car. Elaine commented that that wouldn't have happened in England, to which the men responded, 'Why? What is wrong with your women?'

Another question that is often discussed is whether women make a distinctly female contribution to working life. Should women be represented in all areas of working life because they have something different to input that will be ultimately enriching for the organization, or simply as a matter of justice and equal opportunity because of the similarities that they share with men and because diversity is better for business? More specifically, it is often suggested that women's leadership style differs from men's and so their inclusion in organizational hierarchies will bring skills that were lacking, or will mean that those organizations are better equipped for the changing nature of working life. It's not an easy question to answer. To argue that there is a distinctly feminine way of leading is not very far from the gender essentialism that says men should be scientists and women should be carers. The fact is that some women do lead differently; but others don't. This may be another area where Judith Lorber is correct in saying that we see what we believe, and we assume that our experience is true for all men and all women in all contexts.

## Christian workplaces

Although relatively few people work for churches or Christian organizations, it's worth noting that those who do may have more to negotiate in terms of gender at work because of the range of views within the Church on the roles of men and women. While gender equality within politics and business is accepted as desirable and worth pursuing, particularly in terms of more equal representation of women in leadership roles, in the Church the same issue is a source of conflict and factions. This is perhaps seen most clearly in the prolonged discussions the Church of England has been having about when and how women will become bishops, but it's found across other churches too.

In her studies of gender and organizations Patricia Yancey Martin found that 'the dynamics associated with gender routinely make workers, particularly women workers, feel incompetent, exhausted and/or devalued'.[7] In addition to the usual challenges preventing gender equality within working life, women working for churches and Christian organizations need to negotiate different theological perspectives on what women can and can't do in the church, at home, at work and in public life, adding a layer of complexity that compounds the issues and increases insecurity. Rosie Ward, in *Growing Women Leaders*, finds that 'women who are raised in the evangelical tradition, especially in churches where women's leadership is questioned, find it hard to get away from the internalized question, "Should I really be doing this?"'[8] That nagging doubt can gnaw away at our confidence and limit our effectiveness if we don't address it.

## *Making changes*

Leaders of workplaces have the opportunity to create an environment where equality flourishes. But that's not the only way that change can happen, which is good news for those of us who work in contexts that seem oblivious to gender dynamics. The four avenues for change that I mentioned earlier are also relevant for organizations and workplaces.

- Individual action from one person in the organization
- Collective action where groups work together to challenge gendered aspects of organizational life
- Legislative action that is imposed on organizations from outside
- Organizational action where the organization itself takes initiative for internal change.

There is no one-size-fits-all approach to achieving gender equality within organizations, and evidence would suggest that actions need to take place in different places at the same time in order to bring about lasting change. Let's explore what could be done in each of these areas in turn.

### Individual action

My first job was teaching maths, and in my spare time I got involved in a local youth organization, Bath Youth for Christ, joining their management committee which was predominantly male. The other people on it seemed confident, knowledgeable and full of ideas whereas I was new and quite shy. At one meeting early on, I tried to contribute to the discussion several times, but each time was interrupted by one of the men present who took the conversation off in a different direction. At the end of the meeting I hesitantly and emotionally pointed out what had happened, saying that I just hadn't been heard. To their credit, they listened; we introduced a system for our meetings where if we wanted to say something, we had to raise a hand first. It took a bit of getting used to, but it worked well for that group. This shows how the actions of one person, who in this case was a volunteer, can bring about change.

It would be naive to suggest that that kind of intervention will always be met with such a positive response, but it's worth at least trying. Having a conversation with a line manager might be easier and more productive than addressing a whole group; but while the manager may have the influence to change things, if he or she is unsympathetic you could just be ignored; you need to weigh up which route is more appropriate. Taking action as an individual doesn't mean that you have to go it completely alone. Talk the situation through with friends outside the organization and ask their advice. Find out if you have allies within, even if they don't want to challenge with you. Rehearse what you want to say, and be polite and constructive rather than accusatory.

Some people might want to take action to create for themselves what their workplace is lacking because of its gendered nature. Jude Levermore is a leader in the Methodist Church and often finds that she is the only woman in a room of male colleagues. She meets with a business coach regularly to talk through the issues she faces as a woman in leadership, and actively seeks out female peers from other organizations in order to share experiences with and learn from them.

## Collective action

The film *Made in Dagenham* tells the true story of the women machinists at the Ford car company who went on strike in 1968 in protest at being paid less than men at the factory who were doing work requiring a similar level of skills. The women made car seat covers, so as the stocks of finished covers ran out production at the factory gradually ground to a halt. The strike lasted three weeks and led to the passing of the Equal Pay Act of 1970. It shows how, together, people can confront institutionalized sexism and bring about change when it would be impossible for one person to do it on their own.

## Legislative action

The Equalities Act in 2010 brought together over 100 pieces of legislation to provide a legal framework in which all types of equality can flourish. It protects men and women from direct and indirect discrimination and harassment on the basis of eight protected characteristics, including sex. Men and women should be paid on an equal basis, have the same access to flexible working and undergo the same selection process for jobs. Equalities legislation tries to balance people's rights to hold and live out their beliefs, recognizing the need to end discrimination against particular groups. Certain types of employment are exempt from the act, including priests and ministers of religion, which is why the Church of England can't be prosecuted for sex discrimination by not ordaining women as bishops. But any Christian organization that wanted to restrict senior leadership roles to men would be on dodgy ground if that was challenged in court.

Of course, just having the legislation there doesn't mean that it is adhered to, nor should we assume that Christian organizations are all models of good practice. In 2012, a female lecturer at a Bible college in the north of England discovered that she was being paid a lot less per year than a male colleague who was doing the same role and was less qualified. She raised it with her line manager and was given a justification for her lower pay, but within two days they had increased her salary to the same rate. If you feel that you are discriminated against because of your sex, it's worth taking advice before challenging this behaviour, to find out exactly what your rights are.

## Organizational action

Some organizations choose to address gender equality as a corporate priority. Tearfund is an international relief and development agency with an evangelical Christian foundation. Working to empower women and girls and addressing gender equality issues has long been considered to be best practice in terms of international development work, but Tearfund has also chosen to actively pursue gender equality within their UK headquarters through a number of activities, including policies and guidelines, the appointment of a gender adviser, and a gender audit. While Tearfund themselves would agree that they are on a journey with this issue and are by no means perfect, there's a lot to be learned from their experience.

Strong leadership is key in making organizations more gender equal, and Tearfund's CEO and members of the executive team were actively involved in promoting gender equality. For a time, the organization had a dedicated gender adviser whose job it was to champion and progress gender equality both internationally and within the UK. Any organization needs to invest time, energy and resources into addressing gender equality internally; it doesn't just happen. Tearfund also benefited from having Elaine Storkey, a significant voice for the equality of women and men in the Church, as their President for 16 years. There is a connection in the business world between the presence of women on the board and the number of women in higher leadership positions. Women on the board can be a signifier of an inclusive workplace; they can serve as role models and be 'a powerful antidote to damaging stereotypes that devalue women's abilities'.[9] Although the charity sector is different in many ways from the world of business, the presence of capable women as presidents, vice-presidents and board members, as well as the type of men who serve in those capacities, can be a way of organizations signalling their attitude towards gender equality.

Tearfund found a compelling reason to pursue gender equality. In 2004, the UN discovered that in some African countries the people most at risk of contracting HIV were married women.

Tearfund investigated whether this was true in the Church, and found that in certain places the Church was contributing to the problem through its teaching on how men and women should relate. They set up a pilot project in Zimbabwe and Burkina Faso to address inequality in relationships and to explore what the Bible says about men and women.[10] They found that addressing gender inequality led to measurable benefits in the development of the community – increased testing for HIV, changed sexual behaviour for men and women, an increase in shared responsibility for children and changed attitudes. Promoting gender equality worked. If organizations want to take it seriously, it helps if they can articulate gender equality as part of their core mission.

Tearfund discovered the value of paying attention to the 'saying and doing' of gender through allowing people to tell their stories. Andrew McCracken, one of the executive team, describes a conversation with a female colleague, as part of the gender audit, where it came out that she felt she wasn't listened to because she is a woman. 'I would never have guessed that in a million years', he says, 'because she's confident, a very impressive lady, so I think that helps me work with her better and understand her better which I think makes Tearfund a better place.' Matthew Frost, Tearfund's CEO, referring to how gender equality was measured in the organization, says that 'anecdotes and stories reveal gender bias and enable us to build a picture alongside the audit data'. A fellow director had spoken in a meeting of the executive team about how upset he had been as a man when he heard how a woman had been badly treated at work. Frost says: 'recounting it was very powerful, hearing how she felt at the time. Telling the story means that it lives on.'

Because they are a Christian organization, they also created space for people to talk about their different theological understandings. It is not possible to develop a theology of gender in a context divorced from the day-to-day practisings of gender. Theological beliefs are constructed not by abstract intellectual analysis of Bible texts, but are integrated with, and co-constituted by, people's lived experience. Frost observes, when talking about different Christian views on gender, that 'some of it is belief; an awful lot of it is blindness'. So rather than avoiding theology for fear of creating division, it seems important for Christians who want to address gender equality to make space for people to discuss their theology of gender in a safe context where debate and questions are welcomed and allowed, and to recognize the complexity of the issue.

There are also many ways in which organizations can progress gender equality in smaller stages.

- Improve women's access to jobs, and enhance women's careers, as they are the ones who are disadvantaged in the workplace. Ensure that women have easy access to mentoring or coaching support, looking outside the organization for appropriate mentors if they don't exist within it. Examine job descriptions for gender bias; asking for ten years' previous experience, for example, may favour men, who have not taken maternity leave – is that period of time essential? Actively encourage women to apply for senior roles so that there is a bigger pool of applicants to fish from, while keeping the selection process the same.
- Have family-friendly policies that enable both parents to balance work and family life, without assuming that women will take the main responsibility for their children. Encourage men to take paternity leave when their children are born and consider a more generous provision than the statutory length of time off.
- Challenge sexism through training and awareness-raising, being clear about what is acceptable within the organization. Identify specific training needs that men or women might have; for example, Tearfund runs an annual assertiveness course for women and also one for men on models of success that encourages a more holistic approach to work.

## The wild dream of Christians leading the way

Because paid employment is such a dominant part of so many of our lives, it helps to be aware of how it can affect our experiences of being women and men, and how we can change our workplaces to be ones where equality is valued. My prayer is that Christians will lead the way in creating workplaces where both women and men can thrive and contribute to their full potential, where discrimination and prejudice are eliminated in all their forms, and the empowering leadership that Jesus modelled is valued and replicated.

# 9

## Church and equality

————•◦•————

Paul likened the people of God to a body with many parts,[1] each of which is important and each with something to contribute. If one part of the body is missing, or inactive, or told that it's not needed, or excluded, then the whole body suffers. If every part is the same and there isn't diversity, then the whole body suffers. I wonder what he would say if he could see us now.

Like organizations, churches are gendered institutions, meaning that our experience of what happens there, what we're allowed to do, who's in charge, what's valued and what's frowned on, is different for men and for women. Our churches have been organized, led and controlled by men for centuries, so although there are currently fewer men in our churches, they are not great places for many women to be either. Maggi Dawn is an ordained priest in the Church of England who is now Dean of Chapel and Professor of Theology at Yale Divinity School in the USA. She deliberately chose to leave the Church of England when her previous role as a chaplain in Cambridge came to an end, because the Church was so unwelcoming of women and their contribution. In her book *Like the Wideness of the Sea*, she writes movingly of the rudeness and naked sexism that she endured for many years because she is a woman and a priest. She says about her move to Yale:

> I never anticipated what an absolutely transforming ex-
> perience it would be to be treated automatically as an
> equal. It makes a huge difference on a personal level –
> heart, soul, mind and strength – to work in an environment
> where I am never treated with suspicion just because I am

a woman . . . What I would love my colleagues in the Church of England to know is this: I achieve twice as much in a working week as I did before. Why? Simply for this reason: none of my mental energy is wasted justifying my existence, surviving bullies, fending off harassment or anticipating sexist behaviour.[2]

I have supported and advocated for women in leadership for many years, and in my experience Maggi is far from alone. Many talented, competent women are denied opportunities to use their gifts within the Church and find that environment draining and disempowering.

## *Working towards equality*

How to make our churches places where women, men and children thrive is a huge subject, with layers of complexity, and so in one chapter I can make only a few suggestions. I want to explore some ways in which churches can release the gifts and contributions of women, as that is where my experience lies, and create an environment where all are valued regardless of their sex. I think there needs to be a wider conversation about why there are fewer men in church and what can be done about it. Some of these suggestions need church leaders to take a lead, but all of us have a role to play in asking questions and working towards change.

### Leaders have a key role to play

It might seem an obvious thing to say, but just as in organizations, church leaders are key when it comes to creating an environment where both women and men are able to flourish. Church leaders need to publicly affirm their support for the equality of women and men, rather than assume that everyone knows that's what the church thinks. It's possible to do this while making space for a range of views within the congregation, but being silent on the issue allows confusion to win and stops women from fully participating. Depending on the structure of your church, it might be appropriate to get the PCC or church members to discuss it at a meeting, or to talk about it in church services. If you are unsure about what your church's position is, or if mixed messages are being given, then ask to talk to your church leader about it.

Malcolm Duncan is the lead pastor of Gold Hill Baptist Church in Chalfont St Peter, Buckinghamshire. When he joined, in 2010, he led the church through a process of reconsidering their position on women in ministry.[3] A committed egalitarian, he says:

> It strikes me that to believe in something means that you must live out of that belief – so that is what I have done. I am deeply uncomfortable with the view that you hold a position, but do nothing about it because of fear of what others might say, think or do. So for me, being committed to the view that I hold meant that I could not secretly hold it, but must play my part in advocating it, teaching it, practising it and living it out – albeit within the context of Christian community, sensitivity and seeking not to be an offence to others.

Duncan taught on the equality of women and men, and particularly on women in leadership, encouraging conversation; the church went through nine months of dialogue, prayer and questioning before changing the constitution at a church meeting. A few people were unhappy with the change and left, but overall it has been a very positive move.

## Teach about biblical equality

Churches need to take time to teach from the Bible about the equality of men and women, involving the whole of the church. Miriam Swaffield, who is a student worker with Fusion, says:

> Events and conferences for women teach about equality and the theology behind it, but it won't make much difference unless men's days teach exactly the same. We need whole church teaching on this otherwise we get the women all empowered and fired up, only to hit a wall at home.

This could be done through a sermon series in the main service, which will signal its importance to the whole church, but Bible study groups can easily explore the issue for themselves.

## Have a clear purpose for single-sex groups

Single-sex groups are often set up with good intentions, but as we saw earlier when considering education, they can end up exacerbating stereotypes and not addressing the issues they were created to overcome. A women's Bible study that meets during the daytime may have been started to meet the needs of mums who were not able to attend house groups in the evenings. However, it risks communicating that the church believes that home is where mums should be, and full-time mothers are somehow more important than those who go out to work because, look – they've got a special group. Instead of being a women's group, could it be a Bible study group for those who are free during the day – a subtle but important distinction?

## Be proactive about developing skills and opportunities

It's important to develop the skills of women leaders and to create opportunities for them to use them. Ask the women in your church what they need to grow in leadership and what their aspirations are. What's stopping them from being leaders at the moment? Church leaders should identify women who seem to have an aptitude for leadership and team them up with more experienced women to act as mentors, even if they have to look outside their congregation. Younger or less experienced women leaders should be given opportunities to take on small projects, with support and feedback, and build on that. Encourage women to attend leadership events, read books, or set up a study group where they can talk about issues with others. It's possible that some women will need their confidence built but could be nudged towards a leadership role that they will excel at once they get there. I lead a beginners' running group for my running club, and although it's open to everyone, 90 per cent of the participants are women. Many of them are hesitant to run on their own and assume that they're not good enough to join the club straight away, but after a few sessions there's no stopping them.

## Be intentional about finding women who can speak and lead

Look back over the past year to see who has preached or had upfront roles in your church. Count how many of them are women and how many men. If there's an imbalance, be proactive about addressing it. Although there is much more to creating an equal environment than having women in leadership roles, it does send a powerful signal of inclusion.

Over the years I have often challenged events or churches that don't have women as speakers. Invariably the response is that they just don't know any gifted women. It's a vicious circle – women don't get invited because they don't have experience or aren't known, and they aren't known and have less experience because they aren't given opportunities. The Women's Room[4] is an online directory of women speakers, set up to address the imbalance in the experts used to comment on current affairs in the media – three-quarters of whom are men. Women can register stating their own areas of expertise, and it is now known by the media as a reliable source of competent women who can speak on a wide range of issues. I have often wondered whether we need something similar in the Church, because there is no shortage of women who can preach and teach.

Youthwork Summit is a one-day event for youth workers that has been intentional about working towards an equal number of male and female contributors. Matt Summerfield, executive director of Urban Saints and one of the organizers, says: 'Turning that intention into practice hasn't been easy. We don't want to be tokenistic in any way. And we've invited some women who have turned us down, which has been disappointing.' When selecting speakers he and the team have focused on spiritual maturity and fitness for purpose, deliberately recognizing that leadership comes from gifting and is not related to gender. It's taken the Summit three years to achieve gender parity on their speaking team, and they are keen to continue. If you are looking to increase the number of female contributors to events, it's important to be clear about your criteria for inviting people, and make sure it's not just about who you know. Once you're clear about what qualifies someone to speak, you don't need to lower your standards, but it may be harder to find women who meet them just because they are less well known. Ask around for suggestions and be constantly on the lookout for good women speakers so you have a bigger pool to draw from. There also needs to be a welcoming of different styles of preaching and speaking, so that diversity is valued and modelled.

## Youth and children's work should not perpetuate stereotypes

Once, when I was teaching some youth work students about gender, a male youth worker said that he always asks the boys to put the tables away at the end of the session, while the girls tidy and wash up. Other people in the group challenged his practice. Why shouldn't the girls take their turn in putting away the tables, and the boys get involved in washing up? His response was that 'it just felt right' that boys should do the lifting and carrying, even though the tables were folding ones that actually aren't that heavy. It's not that the girls would be physically unable to move the tables; he believes that there are different roles that girls and boys should fulfil. Men should do the lifting; women should wash up. In that small example, he's communicating gendered expectations, saying something about what boys should be like, and what girls should be like, perpetuating unnecessary stereotypes that squash diversity.

A female youth worker described to me what happens at her youth club on a typical Friday night. The girls arrive and all sit down around a table and paint each other's nails or braid each other's hair. The boys all play football, dominating most of the space and making lots of noise. There's no overlap between the two activities; girls do one thing and boys do something different. Nor is there any critique of the gendered nature of those activities, no discussion about why the girls don't play football, why boys don't paint their nails, or why sex is an organizing category. Of course, the young people are choosing what they do, but it's legitimate to ask how free their choice is given the pressure there often is to fit in with what everyone else does. In that small example, that youth worker is communicating something about what boys do and what girls do; she's helping to construct gender differences.

Youth and children's workers are just one influence on young people; they are not the only ones modelling what it means to be a man or a woman. But it's precisely because youth and children's work values young people in all their diversity, and cares about their well-being, that they need to be aware of how their words and actions can expand or restrict the aspirations of the children they are influencing. If we are to help children and young people to reach their full potential, then we shouldn't have gender-bound restrictions on what that potential might be.

## Overcome the fear of women that excludes

A friend of mine is a vicar. When she arrived in her latest parish, she made an effort to build relationships with other local church leaders, to find out what they were doing and whether opportunities existed to work together. One of the people she contacted was the Baptist minister. When she asked to visit him, he said that he couldn't meet her on her own on principle, because she is a woman, insisting that his wife should be present as well. My friend agreed and his wife sat in the corner like a Victorian chaperone, knitting while they talked.

He is not alone in believing that it is inappropriate for a Christian man and woman to meet without another person being present. High-profile male Christian leaders, particularly in the USA, are very public about the boundaries they set, in order to protect their marriages and reputations, such as making sure the office door is open or someone else is in earshot when they meet with a woman; they will avoid travelling alone with a woman, and eating alone with a woman.[5] A number of male Christian leaders provide an opportunity for a young adult to spend a period of time with them as a kind of intern, learning from their leadership and helping out with tasks such as driving. These opportunities are open only to young men, because if they were open to women, there would be the potential for the relationship to go wrong, or for others to project their own values and assumptions on to the situation.

One leader said to me that it would look totally wrong if he were to turn up at a church to preach with a young woman: 'What would people think?!'

Are these safeguards wise, overcautious, justified, or extreme? I can understand the thinking behind them, and it is devastating when people have affairs. However, I believe that the type of boundaries that state that it is unsafe for a man and a woman to meet in a work context unless the door is open or another person is nearby are excessive and discriminatory, and they disadvantage both women and men. They treat women as a problem, and make it more difficult for women and men to interact because extra arrangements have to be made. They imply that men have very little self-control or professional boundaries, or that there is little trust between husband and wife. They play into the myth of women as sexual temptresses whose intention is to seduce men and lead them astray. They leave women out of important discussions and opportunities for networking in a sphere where relationships are key. They ignore the fact that there are men who are attracted to other men. They allow fear of the other to fester, instead of finding ways to work constructively together. They treat men's experience as the norm and they allow men to retain control of who is allowed into networks and opportunities. They are a block to equality because they make it difficult for men and women to work together. They throw suspicion on innocuous meetings, and inject anxiety into conversations. I believe that they actually increase the possibility of affairs because men and women don't learn how to relate to each other normally or how to deal with temptation and attraction.

In their book *Mixed Ministry*, Sue Edwards, Kelley Mathews and Henry Rogers argue that the foundational way that Christians should relate to each other is as brothers and sisters, because we are part of the same family:

> Healthy faith families, just like biological families, need both men's and women's ideas, gifts and perspectives in order to thrive. Single parents will testify that it's tough being both mum and dad. But many ministries today are like single parent families.

They quote John Ortberg, who says:

> I think too often churches avoid the topic or settle for
> an unbiblical 'strategy of isolation' where men deliberately
> separate themselves from women as a means of temptation
> avoidance. This leads to a loss of biblical community, lost
> opportunities for the development of leadership gifts and
> doesn't even help in avoiding sin.[6]

We need to be wise to the possibility of temptation, of course,
but any boundaries should respect women as adults with a contribution to make, and should be negotiated between women and
men. Boundaries need to facilitate men and women working
together, not put barriers in the way. Instead of making elaborate
arrangements to avoid each other, women and men need to
work on their maturity and emotional health. People who feel
that they are at risk of temptation can put extra accountability in
place without needing to avoid the opposite sex altogether. Those
who are concerned about what others think should decide which
is more important – equality of opportunity or the condemnation
of strangers. It must be possible to model something new rather
than be constrained by outdated and suspicious opinions.

## Other things to consider

- *Use inclusive-language Bibles and songs.* Women often need to
  do mental gymnastics to include themselves in Bible readings
  and songs at church: 'Blessed is the man who does not walk in
  the counsel of the wicked',[7] or 'No power of hell, no scheme
  of man can ever pluck me from his hand',[8] or 'Thou my great
  Father, I thy true son'.[9] The language used here obviously comes
  from an era when the word 'man' meant 'people' as well as
  'a male human being', but times change and this is rarely the
  case any longer. Use a version of the Bible, such as the NRSV,
  that uses inclusive language for people, or the latest NIV, which
  has reviewed carefully all gendered language related to people.[10]
  Audit the songs you use in worship and make changes to any
  with exclusive language; or stop using them if the changes are
  too clunky.

- *Think carefully about how you celebrate Mother's Day and Father's Day.* A friend posted on her Facebook page last March: 'I hate Mothering Sunday because it encourages us to take for granted that women are valued more as mothers than as people, mothers somehow love more than fathers and taking someone out for lunch equates to a year of making use of them. None of this is healthy for men or women.' All kinds of women find Mother's Day difficult – those who are unable to have children, those who don't want children, or those who have lost children – and I think that the same is true for many men and Father's Day. How can you celebrate mothering without idolizing motherhood and with recognition of the pain that is present as well as the joy? It's worth considering more widely what kinds of things get celebrated in church – make sure that it's not just engagements, weddings and new babies. A single friend threw her own party when she completed her Masters course because she knew from experience that her church wouldn't acknowledge it; whereas, if she had got engaged there would have been great excitement. Baby showers often give women an opportunity to encourage the mum-to-be. How could the men in the church encourage and support new dads?
- *If they aren't already, encourage men to get involved with children's groups.* A cultural fear exists around men being involved in children's lives: suspicion that is usually disproportionate and always unhealthy. Children and teenagers need the input of both men and women into their lives, particularly if they don't have involved fathers at home. Good safeguarding policies can allay any fears, and Christians should be actively resisting the demonization of men. Su, who runs the youth and children's work at her church, says: 'I am very conscious that this seems to be an arena that women are drawn to so I have worked to encourage men to join our leadership team and have been reasonably successful. There are not yet equal numbers in this but we want to be intentionally encouraging men so that the children and young people have a perspective that church is for everyone rather than just women.'

## Should you stay or should you go?

If your church is not an environment where the full equality of women and men is affirmed, or if there is ambiguity about its position, it can be uncomfortable. You may need to consider whether you're called to stay there or whether it would be better to find another church community to be part of, where both men and women can use their gifts. Sometimes you can only influence from the inside, though, and I know women in significant positions of leadership at work who have decided to stay in complementarian[11] churches in order to be able to gently ask questions about the church's practice; their presence is a reminder of the diversity of women. If you are in this position, it's helpful to find other contexts in which to develop leadership skills, and to be intentional about seeking out women mentors and friends who can support you and pray for you.

## *Working towards a different future*

In his letter to the Galatians, Paul says that within the children of God 'there is neither Jew nor Gentile, neither slave nor free, nor is there male and female, for you are all one in Christ Jesus'.[12] What is important about a person is not what sex they are but whether they belong to Christ. I long for the day when all our churches are places where people are able to contribute on the basis of their gifts, not whether they are male or female, and the diversity of the family of God is genuinely celebrated. I long for the day when we no longer notice whether someone is male or female, but we simply recognize that they are faithfully using their gifts in the extension of God's kingdom. I long for the day when the Church, instead of being one of the very few places where women are legally excluded, fully embraces both its daughters and its sons and welcomes all that they have to offer. I hope you'll join me in helping to make that a reality.

# *Notes*

---

## Introduction

1 An egalitarian view of the Bible says that men and women were created
in God's image to be equal in every way, and together shared in the
responsibilities of bringing up children and stewarding the creation.
This mutuality and equality were distorted by sin, leading to the subordination of women, the domination of men and a corruption of their
response to the cultural mandate to fill all the earth and subdue the
land. Egalitarians emphasize that Jesus challenged the patriarchy of
his day in the way that he related to women and empowered them, an
example that Christians are to follow. Christians are called to redeem
distorted gender relationships and work together in partnership and full
equality in all areas of life, not just church and family, which will lead
to liberation for both men and women. Women and men can both take
on positions of leadership that they are gifted and equipped for, which
should aim to empower others for service rather than exercise power
over them.

## 1 Exploring equality

1 These sites of inequality are expanded on in Chapter 3 and sources for all
the facts are given there.

2 I was brought up in the Brethren Church with a very different understanding of what the Bible taught about men and women. As an evangelical
in my early twenties, it was really important for me to study the biblical
material on women and men, to understand how to interpret it, and to
realize that what I had imbibed as a teenager was not the only or the
most accurate way of understanding the texts. Not all Christians feel
the need to justify their passion for equality with their reading of the
Bible but, if you are from a tradition that does, I would encourage you
to do that work. There are lots of good books to help you, including
Loren Cunningham and David Joel Hamilton, *Why not Women?* (Seattle,
WA: YWAM Publishing, 2000).

3 Leeds City Council's *Equality Improvement Priorities 2011 to 2015*.

4 Neil Thompson, *Promoting Equality, Valuing Diversity* (Lyme Regis: Russell
House Publishing, 2009).

5 Danny Dorling, *The No-Nonsense Guide to Equality* (Oxford: New Internationalist, 2012).

6 From the ACAS publication *Delivering Equality and Diversity*, 2012.

7 <www.unfpa.org/rights/women.htm>.

8 Genesis 1.27.

9 Christian Aid, *Ctrl+Alt+Shift*, the Gender and Power issue.

10 <www.fawcettsociety.org.uk/equal-pay/>.

11 R. W. Connell, *Gender* (Cambridge: Polity Press, 2002).

12 <www.columbiaspectator.com/2010/09/22/guerrilla-girls-speak-social-injustice-radical-art>.

13 <www.guerrillagirls.com>.

14 Dorling, *No-Nonsense Guide*.

15 <http://rachelheldevans.com/blog/4-common-misconceptions-egalitarianism>.

16 See the chapter on Politics and the Workplace in Deborah Cameron's book *The Myth of Mars and Venus* (Oxford: Oxford University Press, 2008) for more on how women have integrated into House of Commons debates.

17 Ultrarunning involves competing in races that are longer than a marathon (26.2 miles; 42km), usually 50km or more.

18 <www.bbc.co.uk/news/uk-20608039>.

19 Robert Cassen and Geeta Kingdon, *Tackling Low Educational Achievement* (York: Joseph Rowntree Foundation, 2007), available from <www.jrf.org.uk/publications/tackling-low-educational-achievement>.

# 2 What are little girls and boys made of?

1 See John Gray, *Men are from Mars, Women are from Venus* (London: HarperCollins, 1993) and a whole range of publications and products.

2 See her paper 'Believing is Seeing: Biology as Ideology' in *Gender and Society*, 7(4), for example.

3 And almost straight away, we get hit by the complexity of the issues we're discussing. Many of you will know, or are, women who love going to football matches; in 2010, around one in four supporters attending Premier League matches were women. Cyclists such as Bradley Wiggins and Mark Cavendish shave their legs, but take part in gruelling all-male races such as the Tour de France.

4 I talk about men and women in this book but I'm aware that life is more complex than that. There are five physical indicators of what sex we are – our chromosomes, hormones, gonads (the organs that make sperm or eggs), genitals, and other sex-specific reproductive organs such as the prostate in men and the womb in women. When a baby is born, or by using ultrasound when they're in the womb, we can see whether they're male or female just by looking at their genitals because usually

all five indicators of sex are in alignment. However, that's not always the case and around 1 in 100 people's bodies differ in some way from the standard male or female, while around 1 in 2,000 babies are born with atypical genitalia, which means that it's not clear whether they are male or female. These conditions are now referred to as intersex, and they show that it's not that simple to divide humanity into two discrete categories labelled male and female when even our bodies show more diversity than that. For more information go to the website of the Intersex Society of North America <www.isna.org/faq/what_is_intersex>.

5  <http://news.bbc.co.uk/1/hi/uk/3002946.stm>.

6  Heading borrowed from the title of Elaine Storkey's excellent book *Men and Women: Created or Constructed?* (Milton Keynes: Paternoster Press, 2000).

7  R. W. Connell, *Gender* (Cambridge: Polity Press, 2002).

8  Simon Baron-Cohen, *The Essential Difference* (London: Penguin, 2004).

9  For example, see the chapter on Preconceptions and Postconceptions in Cordelia Fine, *Delusions of Gender* (London: Icon Books, 2010).

10  Simone de Beauvoir, *The Second Sex* (1949).

11  Lise Eliot, *Pink Brain, Blue Brain* (London: Oneworld Publications, 2010).

12  Fine, *Delusions of Gender*.

13  Connell, *Gender*.

14  Connell, *Gender*.

15  Although men show only a small advantage in mathematical ability over women and studies on aggression show that the response for men and women depends on circumstances. Unprovoked men have a slight tendency to show higher levels of aggressiveness than women, but when they are provoked, men's and women's reactions are much more similar.

16  Deborah Cameron, *The Myth of Mars and Venus* (Oxford: Oxford University Press, 2008).

17  Genesis 2.19–24.

18  Mairtin Mac an Ghaill, *The Making of Men* (Buckingham: Open University Press, 1994).

19  Stephen Frosch, Ann Phoenix and Rob Pattman, *Young Masculinities* (London: Palgrave Macmillan, 2002).

20  From an article by Oliver Burkeman in *The Guardian* <www.guardian.co.uk/lifeandstyle/2008/apr/26/healthandwellbeing.oliverburkeman>.

21  From a report on the Sophia Network website <http://blog.sophianetwork.org.uk/2010/09/girls-do-better.html>.

22  Here are the Bible references for the different activities. Being a leader with authority – taught with authority, Matthew 7.29 and passed it on to others, Matthew 10.1; being an advocate for small children – welcomed

them, Matthew 19.13 and 14; making plans to celebrate an occasion with friends – Passover, Matthew 26.17–19; crying in public – at Lazarus' grave, John 11.35; taking action out of anger – overturning tables, Matthew 21.11–13; caring for the sick – Matthew 12.15; teaching in church – Luke 4.14–21; spending quality time with friends of own sex – the transfiguration, Mark 9.2; rescuing someone from a hostile situation – woman caught in adultery, John 8.1–11; being a peacemaker in an aggressive situation – at his arrest, Matthew 26.52–56; asking for help – woman at the well, John 4.7; making sure relatives are cared for as they get old – Mary at the cross, John 19.25–27; cooking breakfast – after his resurrection, John 21.9; being a public figure with a following – entry to Jerusalem, Matthew 21.1–11; confronting people for hypocrisy – the Pharisees, Matthew 23.13–39; taking risks – sending out the Twelve, Matthew 10.1–42.

## 3 Exploring inequality

1 Women's Sport and Fitness Foundation, *Backing a Winner: Unlocking the Potential in Women's Sport* (2007/08) <http://old.greatersport.co.uk/files/sports_audit.pdf>.

2 <www.wsff.org.uk/the-challenge/the-challenge>.

3 For example, when Adlington won her first Olympic gold in 2008, much was made of her mother buying her shoes as a reward, and she was dubbed the Imelda Marcos of the British Team by the *Daily Mail* <http://www.dailymail.co.uk/femail/article-1043557/Golden-girl-Rebecca-Adlington-inspired-Olympic-swim-triumph-Jimmy-Choo-promise.html>.

4 <www.guardian.co.uk/lifeandstyle/2012/oct/24/womens-sport-underfunded-ignored-charity-claims>.

5 <www.bbc.co.uk/sport/0/sports-personality/15895642>.

6 <http://foot4ward.co.uk/2011/04/06/virgin-london-marathon-statistics/>.

7 <http://kathrineswitzer.com/about-kathrine/1967-boston-marathon-the-real-story/>.

8 <http://news.bbc.co.uk/sport1/hi/football/women/4603149.stm>.

9 Her retirement statement is well worth reading in full at <http://www.guardian.co.uk/sport/2013/jan/14/nicole-cooke-retirement-statement>.

10 Cancer Research UK, *The Excess Burden of Cancer in Men in the UK* (January 2013), available from <http://publications.cancerresearchuk.org/cancertype/mens>.

11 Office for National Statistics report quoted on CALM website <www.thecalmzone.net/about-calm/>.

12 <www.thecalmzone.net/about-calm/>.

13 Cancer Research UK, *Excess Burden of Cancer in Men.*

14 <www.menshealthforum.org.uk/about-us/20275-why-do-we-need-men%E2%80%99s-health-forum>.
15 Men's Health Forum, *The Gender Equity Project Report* (2006).
16 Men's Health Forum, *Gender Equity Project Report*.
17 Action on Smoking and Health factsheet (March 2013), available from <http://ash.org.uk/files/documents/ASH_106.pdf>.
18 Men's Health Forum, *Gender Equity Project Report*.
19 <www.independent.co.uk/life-style/health-and-families/health-news/bowel-cancer-rates-for-men-rise-by-29-8556279.html>.
20 Cancer Research UK, *Men's Cancer Briefing* (January 2013), available from <http://publications.cancerresearchuk.org/cancerstats/stats_male/menscancerbriefing.html>.
21 <www.bbc.co.uk/news/health-14677505>.
22 <www.guardian.co.uk/commentisfree/2013/jan/23/suicide-rates-men-gender-issue>.
23 The remaining 4 per cent were unidentifiable. Mental Health Foundation, *Fundamental Facts 2007*, available from <www.mentalhealth.org.uk/content/assets/PDF/publications/fundamental_facts_2007.pdf>.
24 <http://www.thecalmzone.net/about-calm/press-media-area/achievements-case-studies/>.
25 Mental Health Foundation, *Fundamental Facts 2007*.
26 <http://news.sky.com/story/1068998/huge-problem-of-male-suicide-rate-in-uk>.
27 <www.guardian.co.uk/lifeandstyle/2011/dec/04/why-british-public-life-dominated-men>.
28 Centre for Women and Democracy, *Sex and Power: Who Runs Britain* (2013), available from <www.cfwd.org.uk/uploads/Sex%20and%20Power%202013%20FINALv2%20%20pdf.pdf>.
29 You can find the global league table on the website of the Inter-Parliamentary Union <http://www.ipu.org/wmn-e/classif.htm>.
30 Lord Davies et al., *Women on Boards Report* (2011), available at <www.gov.uk/government/uploads/system/uploads/attachment_data/file/31480/11-745-women-on-boards.pdf>.
31 Lord Davies et al., *Women on Boards*.
32 <www.guardian.co.uk/women-in-leadership/2013/apr/17/leadership?INTCMP=SRCH>.
33 Lord Davies et al., *Women on Boards*.
34 Catalyst, *Women in Leadership: A European Business Imperative* (2002).
35 <www.guardian.co.uk/lifeandstyle/2008/mar/06/women.discrimination atwork>.
36 <www.guardian.co.uk/business/2010/jun/10/virginia-bottomley-interview>.

37  Janet Davis, *My Own Worst Enemy* (Bloomington, MN: Bethany House, 2012).

38  <www.guardian.co.uk/lifeandstyle/2011/dec/04/why-british-public-life-dominated-men>.

39  <www.bbc.co.uk/news/education-14661746>.

40  <www.guardian.co.uk/education/2011/aug/25/girls-gcse-gender-gap-16>.

41  <www.guardian.co.uk/education/datablog/2013/jan/29/how-many-men-and-women-are-studying-at-my-university>.

42  <www.cypnow.co.uk/cyp/news/1046479/belief-girls-school-hinder-boys-performance-study>.

43  There were three publications from the initiative: *The Gender Agenda Final Report*, *Gender and Education – Mythbusters* and *Gender Issues in School: What works to improve achievement for boys and girls*. They are available on the Digital Education Resource Archive of the Institute for Education <www.dera.io.ac.uk>.

44  *Gender Issues in School* (London: DCSF, 2009).

45  Stephen Frosch, Anne Phoenix and Rob Pattman, *Young Masculinities* (London: Palgrave Macmillan, 2002).

46  Research by the NSPCC and the University of Bristol <www.bristol.ac.uk/news/2009/6524.html>.

47  <http://brightonmanplan.wordpress.com/2012/01/19/male-victims-of-domestic-violence-suffering-in-silence-summary/>.

48  Women's Aid factsheet, available from <www.womensaid.org.uk>.

49  <http://mensconferenceuk.wordpress.com/2013/07/09/why-we-have-to-make-crime-a-mens-issue/>.

50  <www.fawcettsociety.org.uk/issue/crime-and-justice/>.

51  Jacinta Ashworth and Ian Farthing, *Churchgoing in the UK* (London: Tearfund, 2007).

52  Although, of course, men have been tailors and fishermen have sewed nets for centuries. It seems that it's more acceptable for men to sew for their livelihood, but not as a hobby.

## 4 Addressing inequality

1  Patricia Yancey Martin, '"Said and Done" versus "Saying and Doing": Gendering Practices, Practicing Gender at Work', in *Gender and Society* 17(3) (2003).

2  All names have been changed.

3  Michael Kimmel, *Why Men Should Support Gender Equality*, MARC (6 June 2012).

4  The source of the quote discussed here is <www.gandhitopia.org/forum/topics/a-gandhi-quote>.

5  This story originally appeared on Ruth's blog <http://ruthwells.wordpress. com/>.

6  John 13.1–5.

7  Her name has been changed.

8  Rebecca Asher, *Shattered* (London: Harvill Secker, 2011).

9  Christine Barter, Melanie McCarry, David Berridge and Kathy Evans, *Partner Exploitation and Violence in Teenage Intimate Relationships* (September 2009), available at <www.nspcc.org.uk/inform/research/findings/partner_ exploitation_and_violence_wda68092.html>.

10  <www.theguardian.com/commentisfree/2013/aug/09/struggle-sexism-man-twitter-misogyny-battle>.

11  <http://steverholmes.org.uk/blog/?p=7031>.

# 5 Home life and equality

1  <http://davidwestlake.wordpress.com/2011/04/08/of-bathrooms-and-childcare/>.

# 6 Marriage and equality

1  Her name has been changed.

2  Kathy Keay (ed.), *Men, Women and God* (London: Marshall Pickering, 1987).

3  1 Corinthians 7.4.

4  Ephesians 5.2.

5  Ephesians 5.21.

6  Ephesians 5.25.

7  Ephesians 5.22.

8  From the comments section of this blog post <http://rachelheldevans. com/blog/4-common-misconceptions-egalitarianism>.

9  Nicky and Sila Lee, *The Marriage Book* (London: Alpha International, 2009).

10  More at <http://blog.sophianetwork.org.uk/2009/12/interview-with-lowell-sheppard.html>.

# 7 Parenting and equality

1  These areas are adapted from Marc and Amy Vachon's definition of equally shared parenting as 'The purposeful practice of two parents sharing equally in the domains of child-raising, housework, breadwinning, and time for self' from their website <http://equallysharedparenting. com>. They have some useful scales for each of their domains: <http:// equallysharedparenting.com/Toolbox.htm>.

2 Proverbs 31.10–31.
3 Find out more at the Gov.uk website <www.gov.uk/paternity-pay-leave>.
4 Find out more at the Gov.uk website <www.gov.uk/flexible-working/overview>.
5 <www.theguardian.com/money/2011/oct/25/stay-at-home-dads-fathers-childcarers>.
6 Still available from <www.fridgemagic.com/praxis.php/catalog/category/view/11>.
7 Campaign website <www.lettoysbetoys.org.uk>.
8 <www.lettoysbetoys.org.uk/thats-for-girls-and-thats-for-boys/>.
9 Martin Saunders wrote this piece when he was editor of *Youthwork* magazine; he is now creative director of Youthscape.

## 8 Work and equality

1 Joan Acker, 'From Sex Roles to Gendered Institutions', in *Contemporary Sociology* 21(5) (1992).
2 Joan Acker, 'Hierarchies, Jobs, Bodies: A Theory of Gendered Institutions', in *Gender and Society* 4(2) (1990).
3 Acker, 'Hierarchies, Jobs, Bodies'.
4 Patricia Yancey Martin, '"Said and Done" versus "Saying and Doing": Gendering Practices, Practicing Gender at Work', in *Gender and Society* 17(3) (2003).
5 From her speech at the World Economics Forum in January 2013.
6 F. M. Wilson, *Organizational Behaviour and Gender* (Abingdon: Ashgate Publishing, 2003).
7 Patricia Yancey Martin, 'Practising Gender at Work: Further Thoughts on Reflexivity', in *Gender, Work and Organization* 13(3) (2006).
8 Rosie Ward, *Growing Women Leaders* (London: BRF, 2006).
9 L. Joy, *Advancing Women Leaders* (Catalyst, 2008).
10 *Gender, HIV and the Church*, available from Tearfund.

## 9 Church and equality

1 Corinthians 12.12–31.
2 Maggi Dawn, *Like the Wideness of the Sea* (London: Darton, Longman and Todd, 2013).
3 Interview at <http://blog.sophianetwork.org.uk/2012/07/interview-with-malcolm-duncan.html>.
4 <http://thewomensroom.org.uk/>.
5 For example, see Michael Hyatt's list, former CEO of Thomas Nelson publishers <http://michaelhyatt.com/what-are-you-doing-to-protect-your-marriage.html>.

6 Sue Edwards, Kelley Mathews and Henry J. Rogers, *Mixed Ministry: Working Together as Brothers and Sisters in an Oversexed Society* (Grand Rapids, MI: Kregel, 2008).
7 Psalm 1.1.
8 From the hymn 'In Christ Alone' by Stuart Townend and Keith Getty.
9 From the hymn 'Be Thou my Vision, O Lord of my heart'.
10 Using inclusive language for God that recognizes the female imagery for God in the Bible is a different but related issue and one you could also consider, although many people find this more controversial.
11 The complementarian view says that men and women were created equal in God's sight but they are essentially different in character and in the roles they are to fulfil. There is a God-given order to marriage, family and church life, with men expected to lead their families and women to submit to their husband's 'headship' in order to fulfil their role as helper. This natural order has been distorted by sin so that men dominate and oppress women, and women usurp authority and strive to be equal with men in every way, but Christians are to resist this. Some complementarians believe that women should not speak publicly or preach in church and that the only positions of leadership that should be open to them are in working with other women or with children; women should not be in positions of authority over men. Others are happy for women to contribute to church life in different ways and to take some leadership roles as long as there is a man in overall leadership or authority over them.
12 Galatians 3.28.

# Bibliography

Listed here are some of the books on equality, gender and theology that have shaped my thinking.

M. Alvesson and Y. D. Billings, *Understanding Gender and Organisations*, London: Sage, 2009.

Rebecca Asher, *Shattered: Modern Motherhood and the Illusion of Equality*, London: Harvill Secker, 2011.

Kenneth E. Bailey, *Paul through Mediterranean Eyes*, London: SPCK, 2011.

Kat Banyard, *The Equality Illusion*, London: Faber and Faber, 2010.

Simon Baron-Cohen, *The Essential Difference*, London: Penguin, 2004.

Gilbert Bilezikian, *Beyond Sex Roles*, Grand Rapids, MI: Baker Academic, 2006.

Deborah Cameron, *The Myth of Mars and Venus*, Oxford: Oxford University Press, 2007.

R. W. Connell, *Gender*, Cambridge: Polity Press, 2002.

Steven Croft and Paula Gooder, *Women and Men in Scripture and the Church*, London: Canterbury Press, 2013.

Loren Cunningham and David Joel Hamilton, *Why Not Women?*, Seattle, WA: YWAM, 2000.

Janet Davis, *My Own Worst Enemy*, Bloomington, MN: Bethany House, 2012.

Maggi Dawn, *Like the Wideness of the Sea*, London: Darton, Longman and Todd, 2013.

Daniel Dorling, *Injustice: Why Social Inequality Exists*, Bristol: Policy Press, 2011.

Danny Dorling, *The No-Nonsense Guide to Equality*, Oxford: New Internationalist, 2012.

Sue Edwards, Kelley Mathews and Henry J. Rogers, *Mixed Ministry: Working Together as Brothers and Sisters in an Oversexed Society*, Grand Rapids, MI: Kregel, 2008.

Lise Eliot, *Pink Brain, Blue Brain*, London: Oneworld Publications, 2010.

Cordelia Fine, *Delusions of Gender*, London: Icon Books, 2010.

Stephen Frosch, Ann Phoenix and Rob Pattman, *Young Masculinities*, London: Palgrave Macmillan, 2002.

Lis Goddard and Clare Hendry, *The Gender Agenda*, Nottingham: IVP, 2010.

# Bibliography

Paula Gooder, *Searching for Meaning*, London: SPCK, 2008.

Arlie Russell Hochschild, *The Time Bind: When Work Becomes Home and Home Becomes Work*, New York: Owl Books, 2001.

Gretchen Gaebelein Hull, *Equal to Serve*, London: Scripture Union, 1989.

Allan G. Johnson, *The Gender Knot: Unravelling our Patriarchal Legacy*, Philadelphia: Temple University Press, 2005.

Kathy Keay (ed.), *Men, Women and God*, London: Marshall Pickering, 1987.

Nicky and Sila Lee, *The Marriage Book*, London: Alpha International, 2009.

Mairtin Mac an Ghaill, *The Making of Men*, Buckingham: Open University Press, 1994.

Scot McKnight, *Junia is Not Alone*, Englewood, CO: Patheos Press, 2011.

David Murrow, *Why Men Hate Going to Church*, Nashville, TN: Nelson Books, 2005.

Ian Paul, *Women and Authority: The Key Biblical Texts*, Cambridge: Grove Books, 2011.

Sara Wenger Shenk, *And Then There Were Three*, Sevenoaks: Spire, 1989.

Elaine Storkey, *Men and Women: Created or Constructed – The Great Gender Debate*, Milton Keynes: Paternoster Press, 2000.

Elaine Storkey, *What's Right with Feminism*, London: SPCK, 1985.

Neil Thompson, *Promoting Equality, Valuing Diversity*, London: Russell House Publishing, 2009.

Phyllis Trible, *Texts of Terror*, London: SCM Press, 2002.

Mary Stewart Van Leeuwen (ed.), *After Eden: Facing the Challenge of Gender Reconciliation*, Milton Keynes: Paternoster Press, 1993.

Natasha Walter, *Living Dolls: The Return of Sexism*, London: Virago, 2010.

Natasha Walter, *The New Feminism*, London: Little Brown, 1998.

Rosie Ward, *Growing Women Leaders*, London: BRF, 2008.

Richard Wilkinson and Kate Pickett, *The Spirit Level: Why Equality Is Better for Everyone*, London: Penguin, 2010.

Naomi Wolf, *The Beauty Myth*, London: Vintage Books, 1991.